VINTAGE WOMEN ADULT COLORING BOOK #12

VINTAGE SHOES

48 PAGES OF FASHIONABLE WOMEN'S FOOTWEAR
FROM THE 20TH CENTURY

I0756058

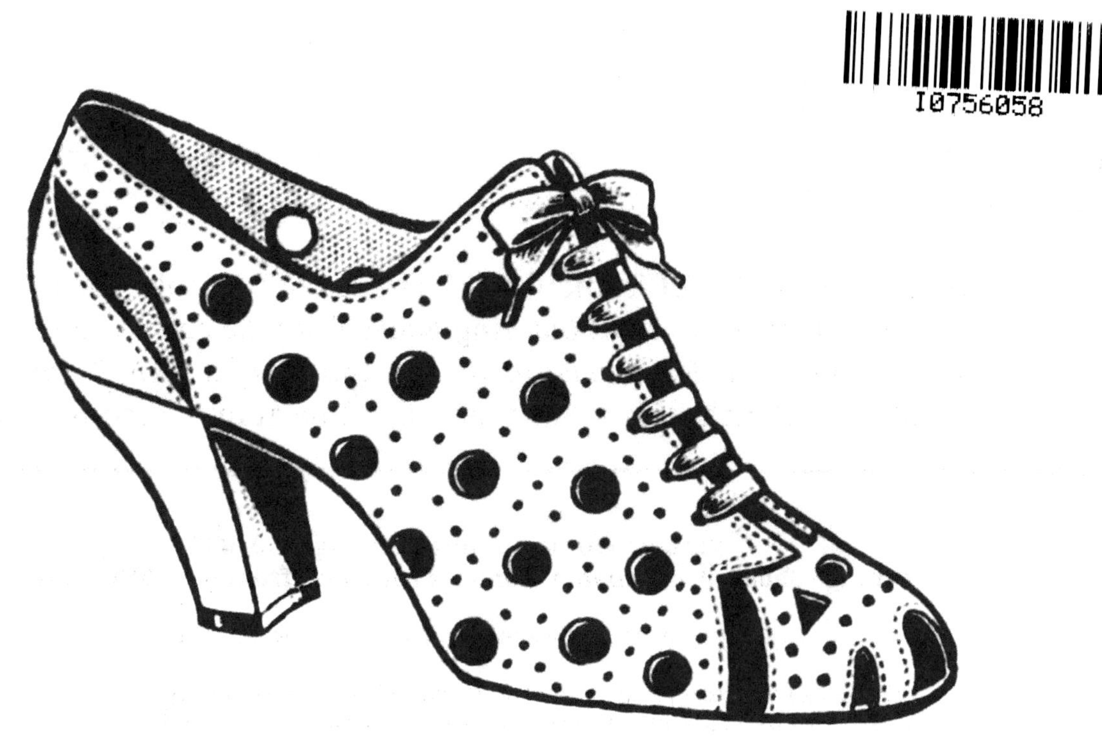

FROM THE EDITORS OF CLICK AMERICANA®
CLICKAMERICANA.COM

INTRODUCTION BY NANCY J. PRICE
EDITOR-IN-CHIEF, MYRIA.COM

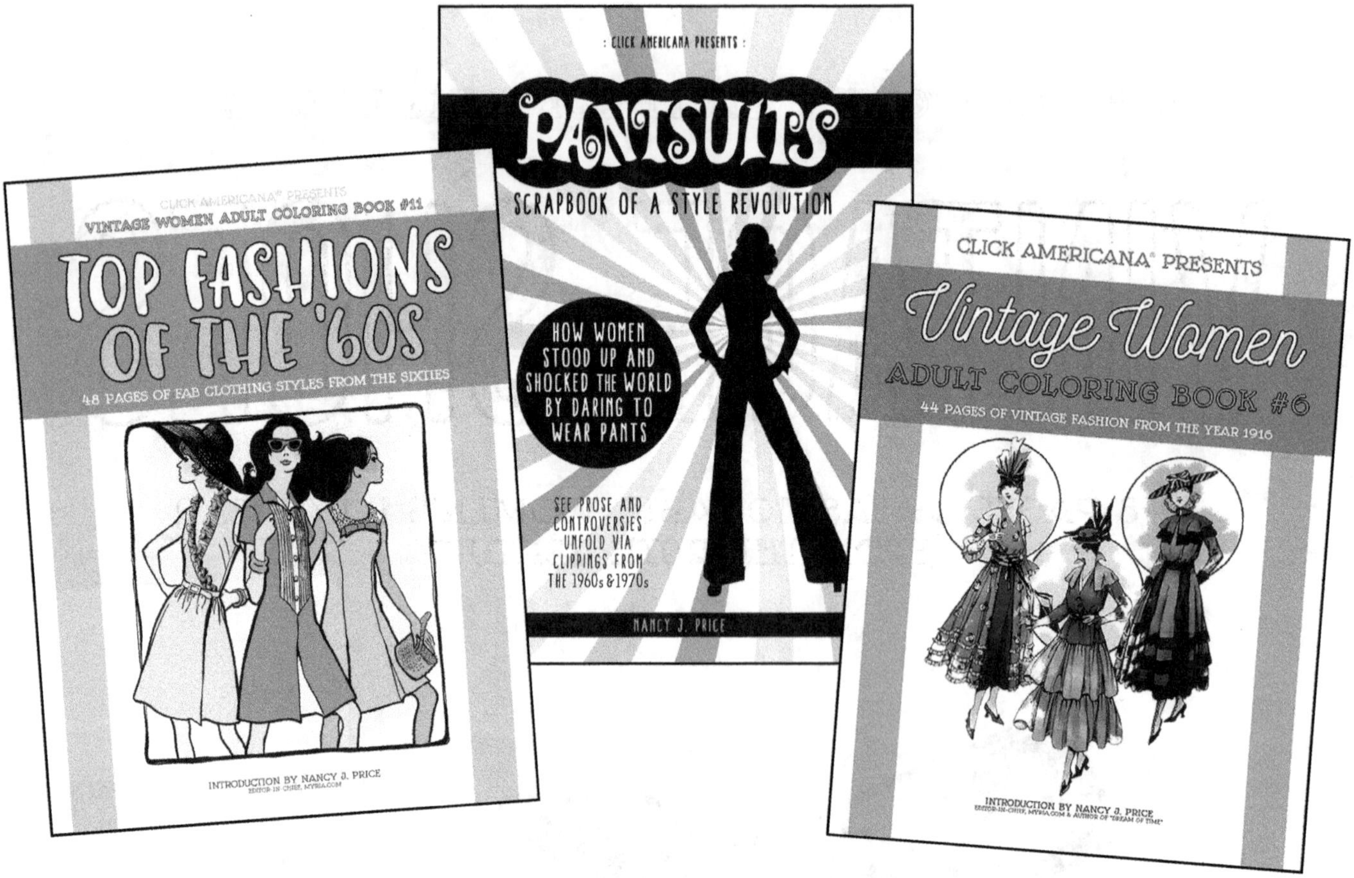

If you're also a fan of fashion, check out our other books, including *Vintage Women Adult Coloring Books from the early 1900s*, *Top Fashion of the '60s* and *Pantsuits: Scrapbook of a Style Revolution* — all from Synchronista. See them all online at myria.com/shop

---

Vintage Women: Adult Coloring Book #12
Vintage Shoes - Fashionable Women's Footwear from the 20th Century

Published by Synchronista LLC – Gilbert, Arizona, USA

www.Synchronista.com

See more books at ClickAmericana.com/shop

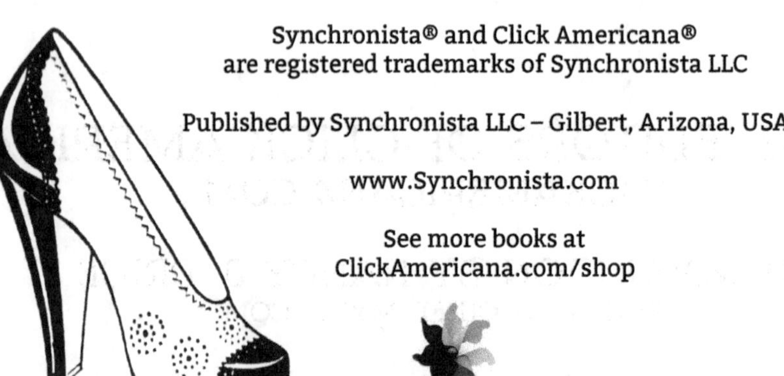

INTRODUCTION

Follow along with the footwear fashions of the 20th century! On the pages inside, you'll see how the most popular women's shoes transformed from being simply utilitarian into truly stylish statements.

We have compiled a fabulous collection of some of the gorgeous boots, booties, heels, pumps, sandals, wedges and loafers that have adorned women's feet over the course of seven decades.

The drawings are arranged by year, first moving from prim high boots to bootie-type heels during the first half of the twentieth century. Then you will see how sleek, pointy-toed stiletto heels became all the rage in the fifties, before eventually giving way to styles like the wide loafers, platform shoes and Bohemian sandals that were so popular in the sixties and seventies.

Each of the images on the 48 pages inside was chosen from thousands of fashion illustrations — the simple, the ornate, and the many looks in between — published between 1907 and 1976. Some drawings are more basic, while others revisit fanciful ad displays of fashion footwear. They're all printed on just one side of the paper, while page numbering and other image information appears on the reverse, ensuring the coloring side is distraction-free and suitable for framing.

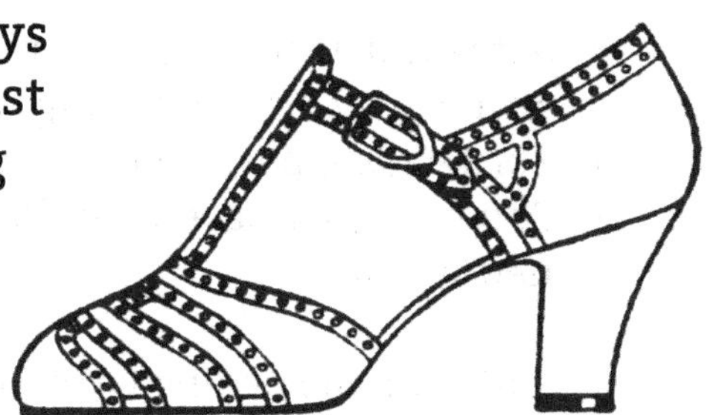

Now, put your best foot forward and color this set of 150 different vintage and retro shoes in your very own style!

Best,

Nancy J. Price
Founder, Click Americana
Editor-in-Chief, Myria.com

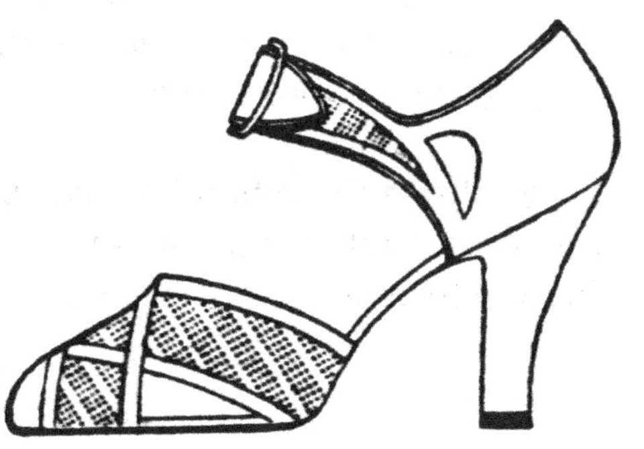

IMPORTANT NOTES

Within these covers, dozens of authentic vintage fashion portraits of women have been rediscovered and transformed into coloring pages. Every one of the retro images in this book was carefully chosen, then painstakingly restored by hand using modern technology in order to return it to its original glory as much as possible.

Before creating this collection, we reached out to coloring book fans, and incorporated as many of their suggestions as we could:

- Each detailed retro picture is printed only on one side of the paper, allowing you to color with your choice of medium without worrying about bleed-through to an image on the back. (If you like, slip a blank page from the end of the book behind the picture you're coloring to avoid ink or paint bleeding onto the next illustration.)
- Page numbering, titles and other image information appears on the reverse of each page, ensuring the coloring side is distraction-free and suitable for framing.

Although these pictures were not created with colored pens, pencils, crayons or paints in mind, we reviewed hundreds of drawings to select those most suited to the task. Still, due to the authentic vintage nature of the artwork, this isn't a typical adult coloring book of modern images with pristine lines.

The images were restored as faithfully as possible, but since the original artwork is not known to exist, we relied upon high-resolution scans of the printed newspaper pages. As such, there are a few caveats:

- Some illustrations have areas of black, including in backgrounds, accessories, and stripes and other clothing design elements.
- Borders, shapes and lines are occasionally incomplete.
- Some details have been lost due to printing processes and quality of preserved newsprint.

In addition, in keeping with the original designs, you will also see...

- There's an sketch-like quality on some illustrations, particularly near the edges or on in areas such as the hair.
- We chose not to over-simplify the majority of the artwork because of the detail (and personality) that would be lost in the process.

We hope these hand-drawn snapshots of history in the making inspire your muse — and we would love to see how you bring color to these beautiful vintage women! You're invited to post your creations on the book's Amazon.com page. Thank you!

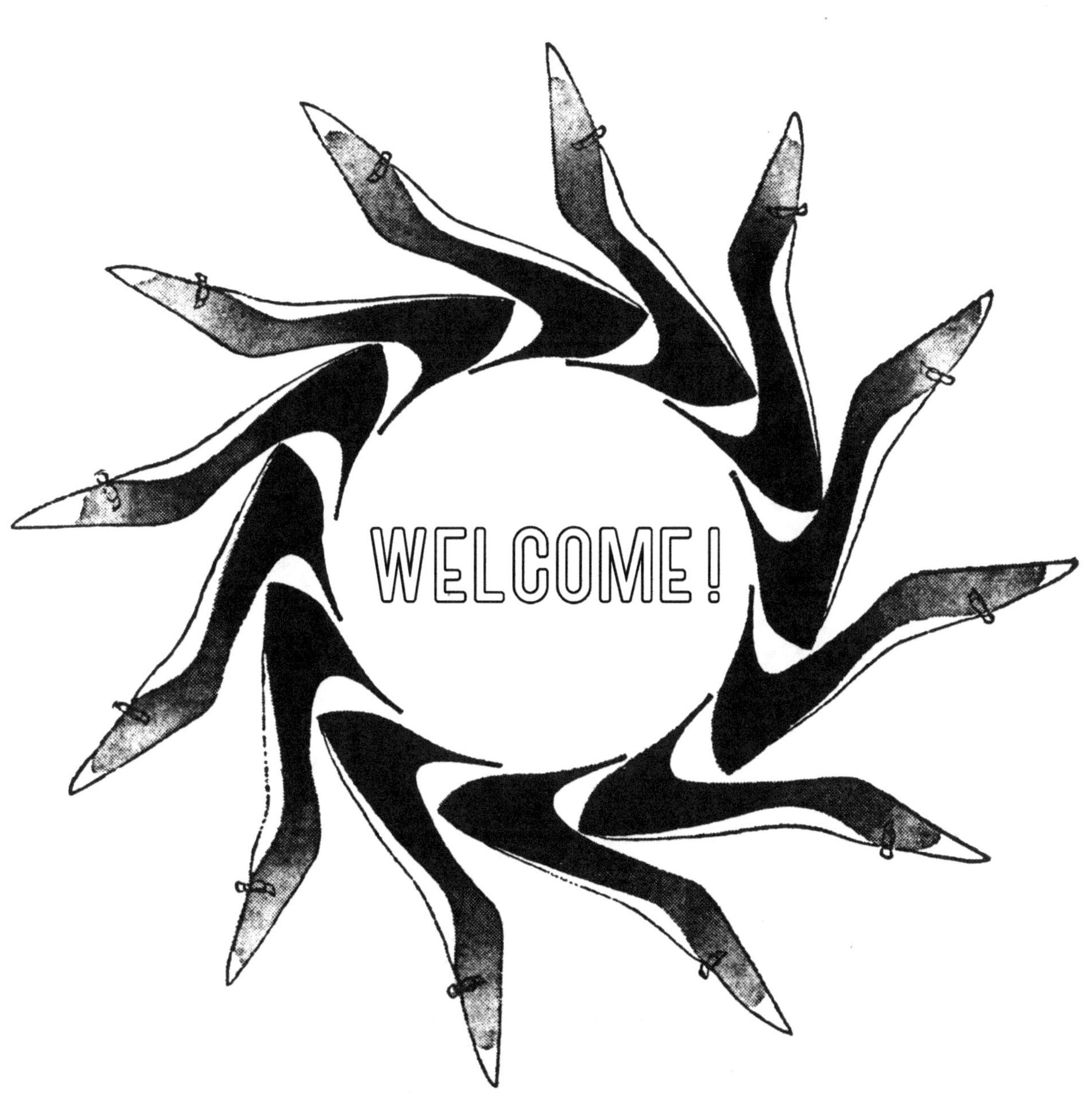
WELCOME!

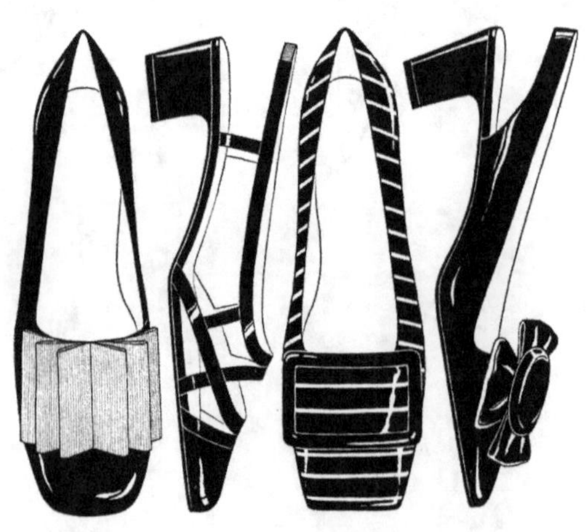

Tip: Find the details about the following illustrations in this space on the back of each page

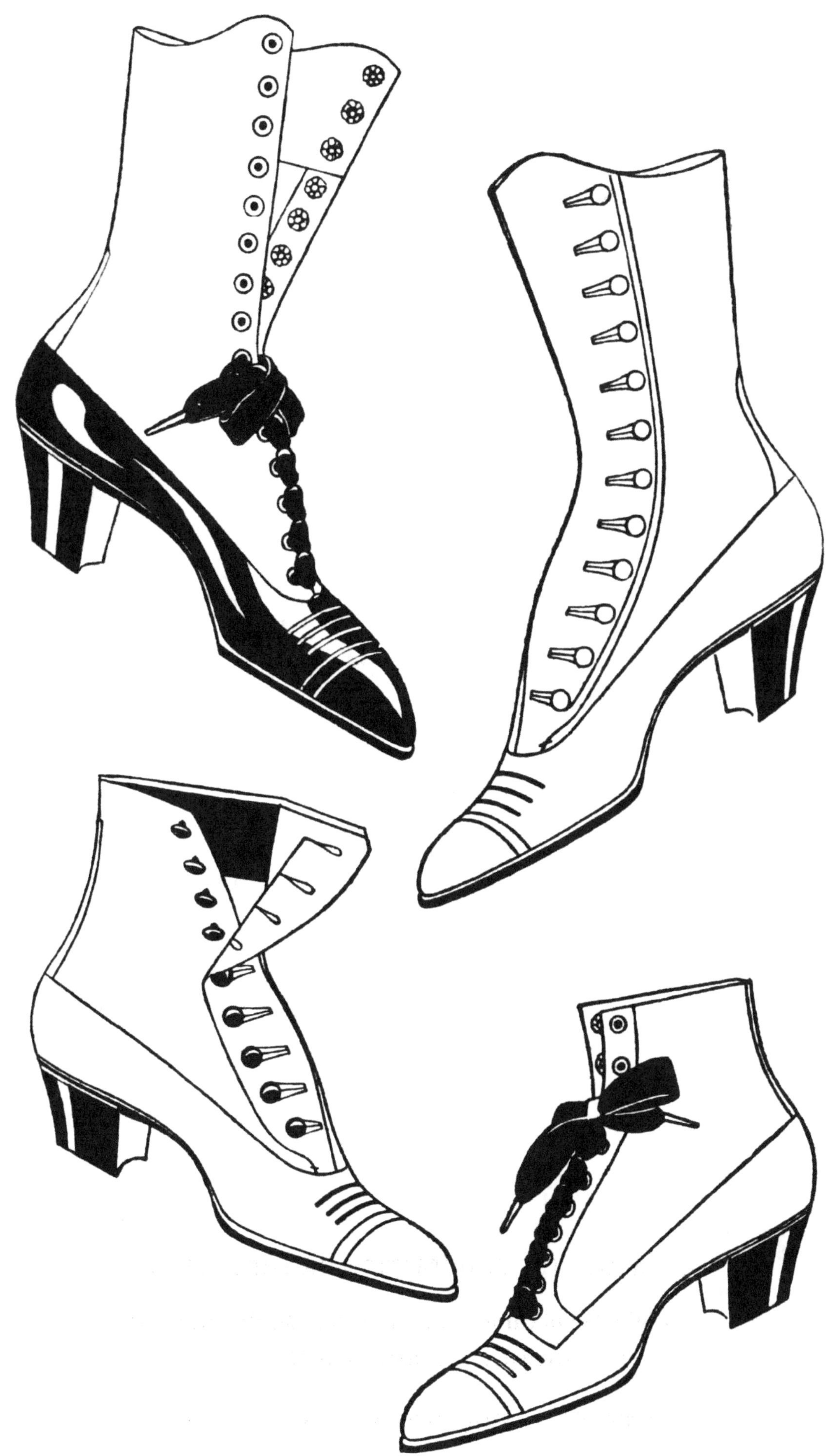

ABOUT THE ILLUSTRATION ON THE REVERSE

Original publication: Evening Star (Washington, DC)
Publication date: October 6, 1907

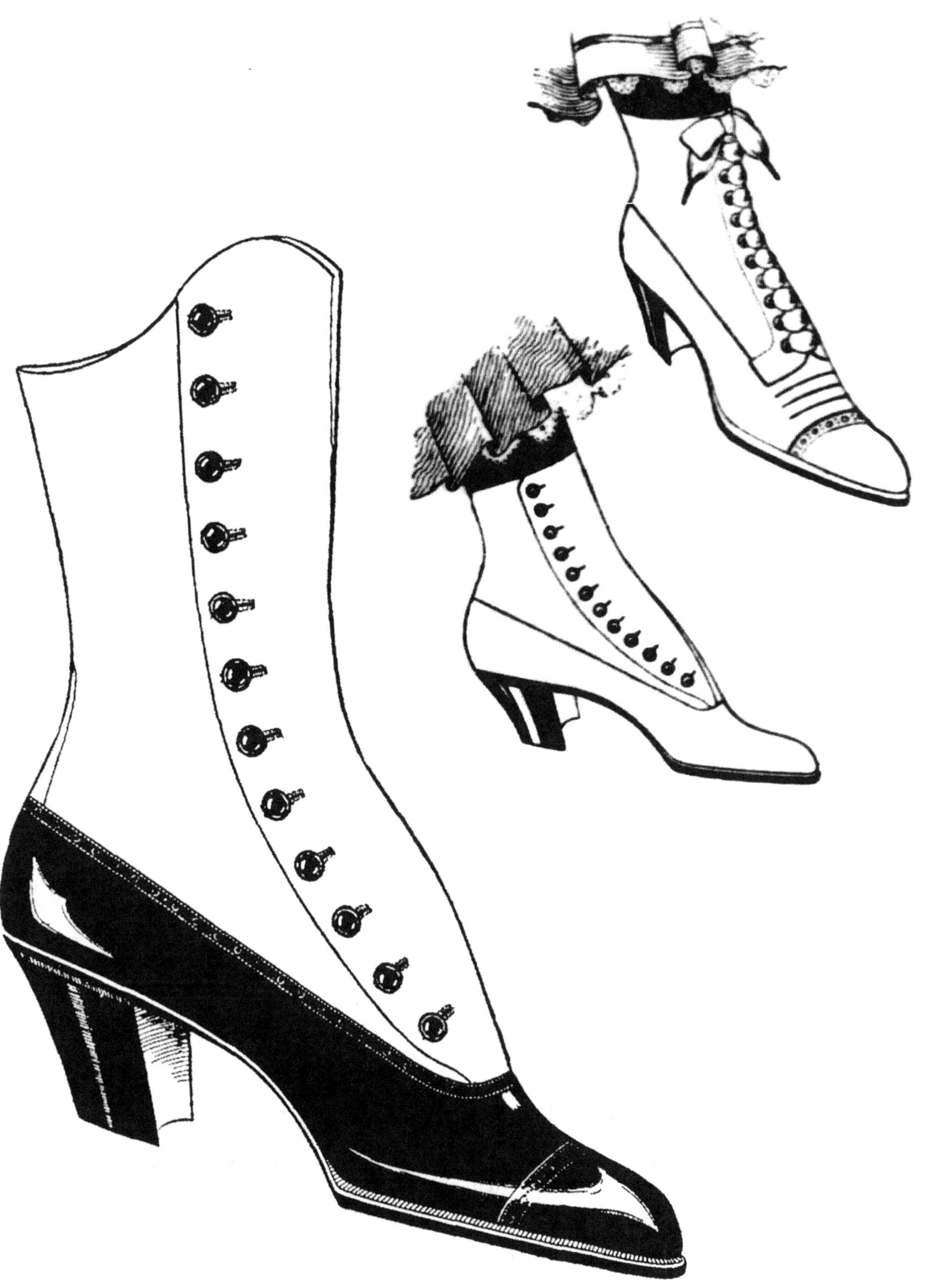

ABOUT THE ILLUSTRATION ON THE REVERSE

Original publication: Washington Post (DC) & Times-Democrat (Lima, Ohio)

Publication date: Oct 10, 1909 & Nov 10, 1907

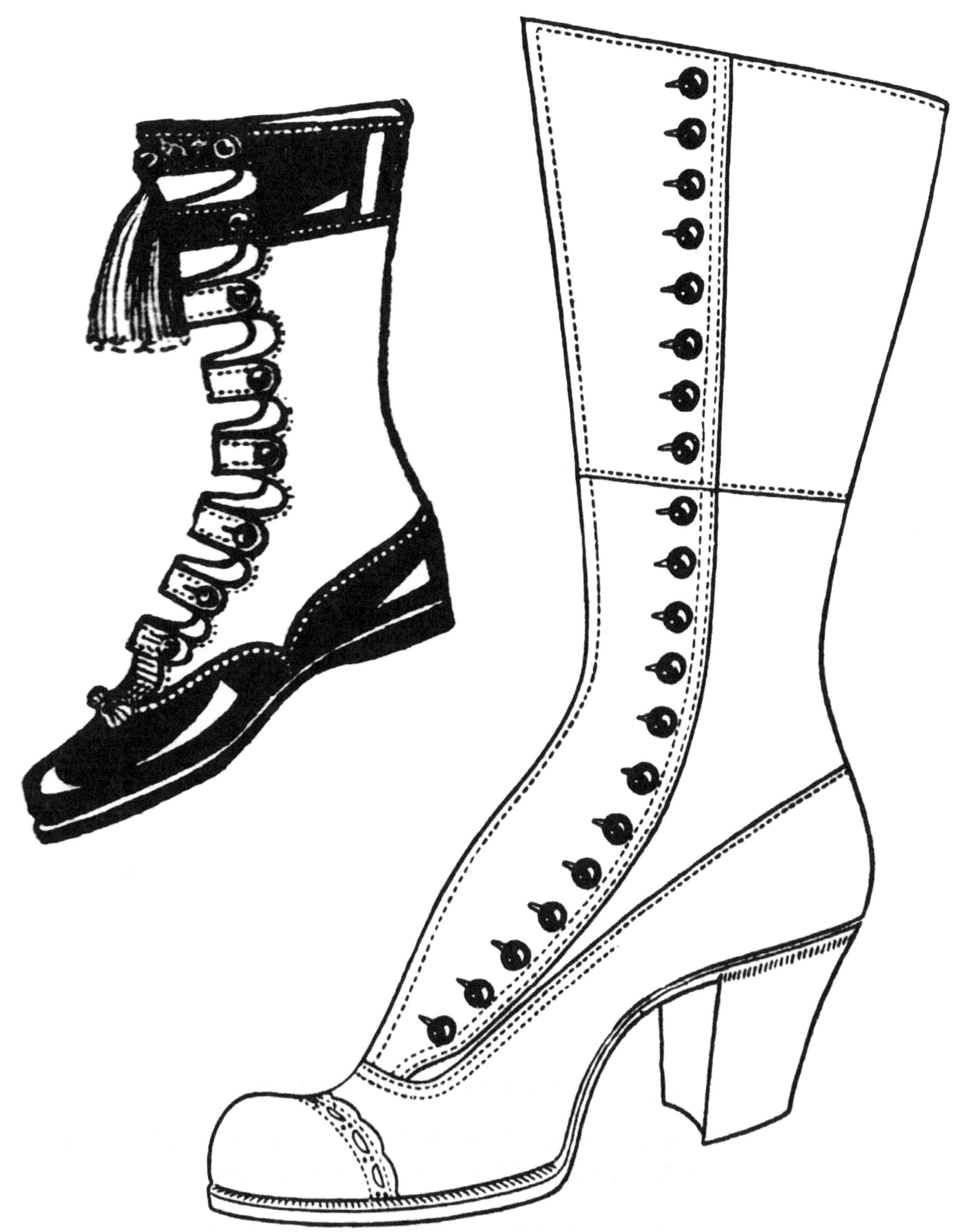

ABOUT THE ILLUSTRATION ON THE REVERSE

Original publication: El Paso Herald (Texas) & Washington Times (DC)
Publication date: July 19, 1911 & September 1, 1912

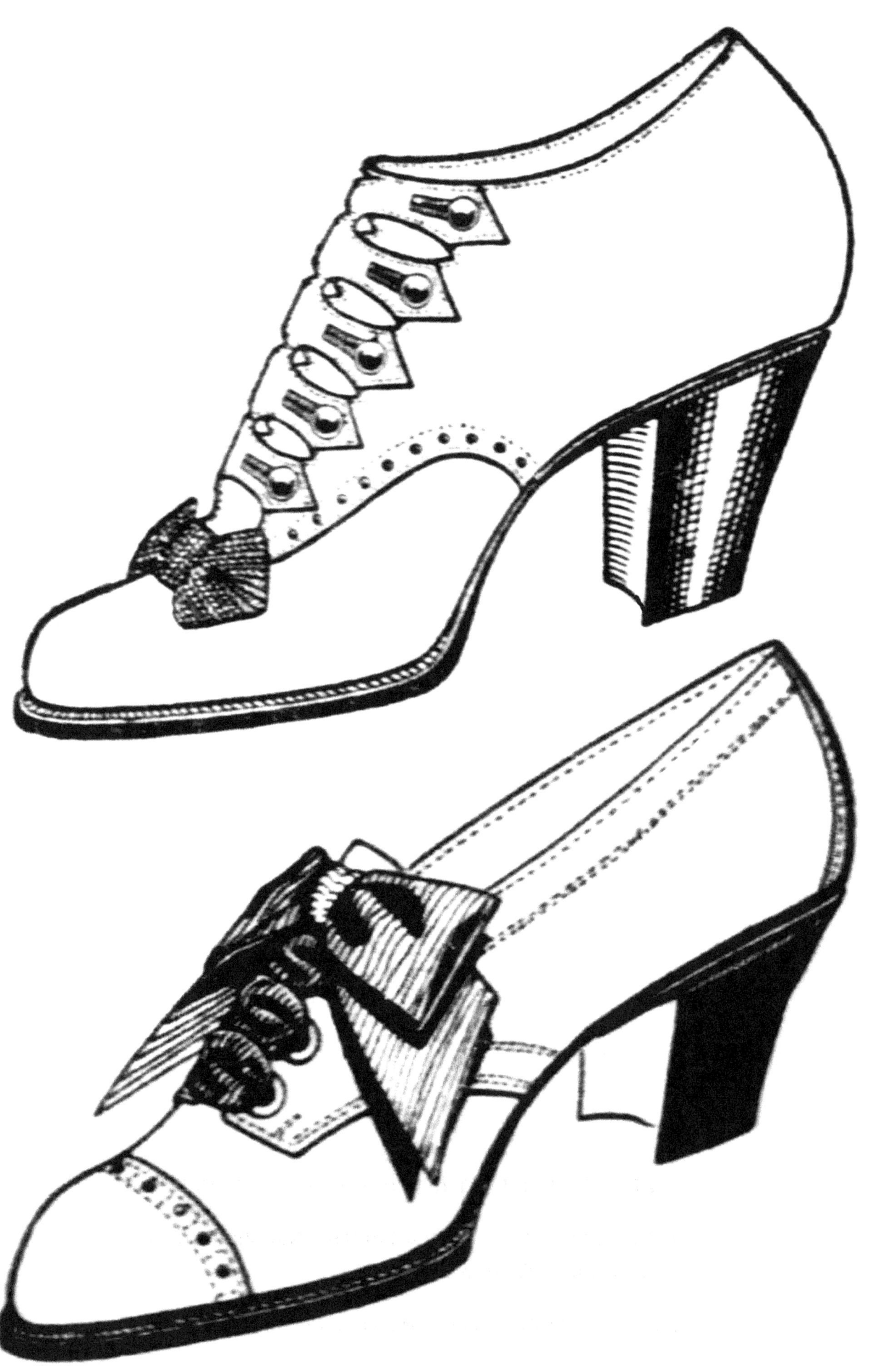

ABOUT THE ILLUSTRATION ON THE REVERSE

Original publication: Manhattan Daily Nationalist (NY)
Publication date: March 14, 1913

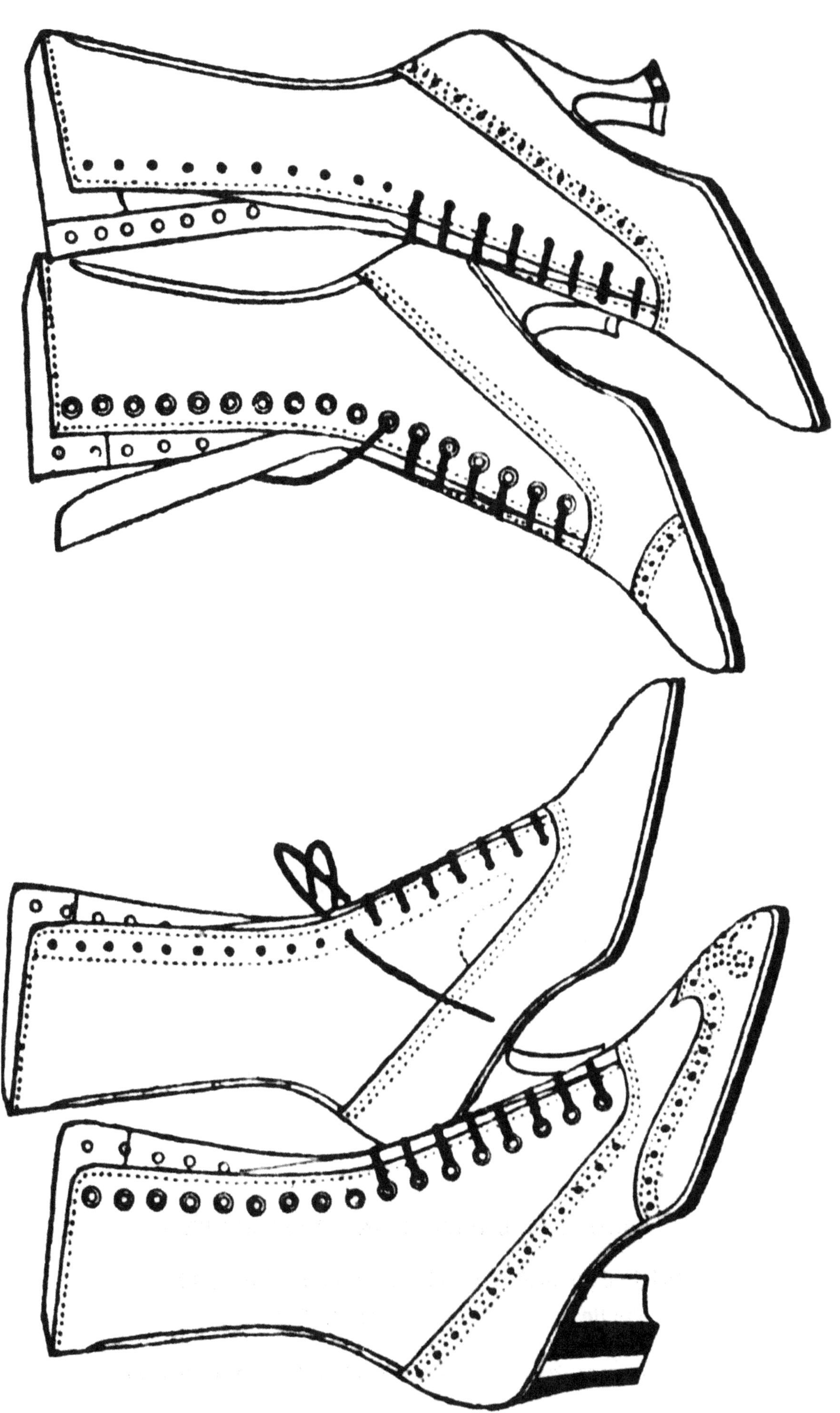

ABOUT THE ILLUSTRATION ON THE REVERSE

Original publication: St Louis Star and Times (MO)
Publication date: December 11, 1921

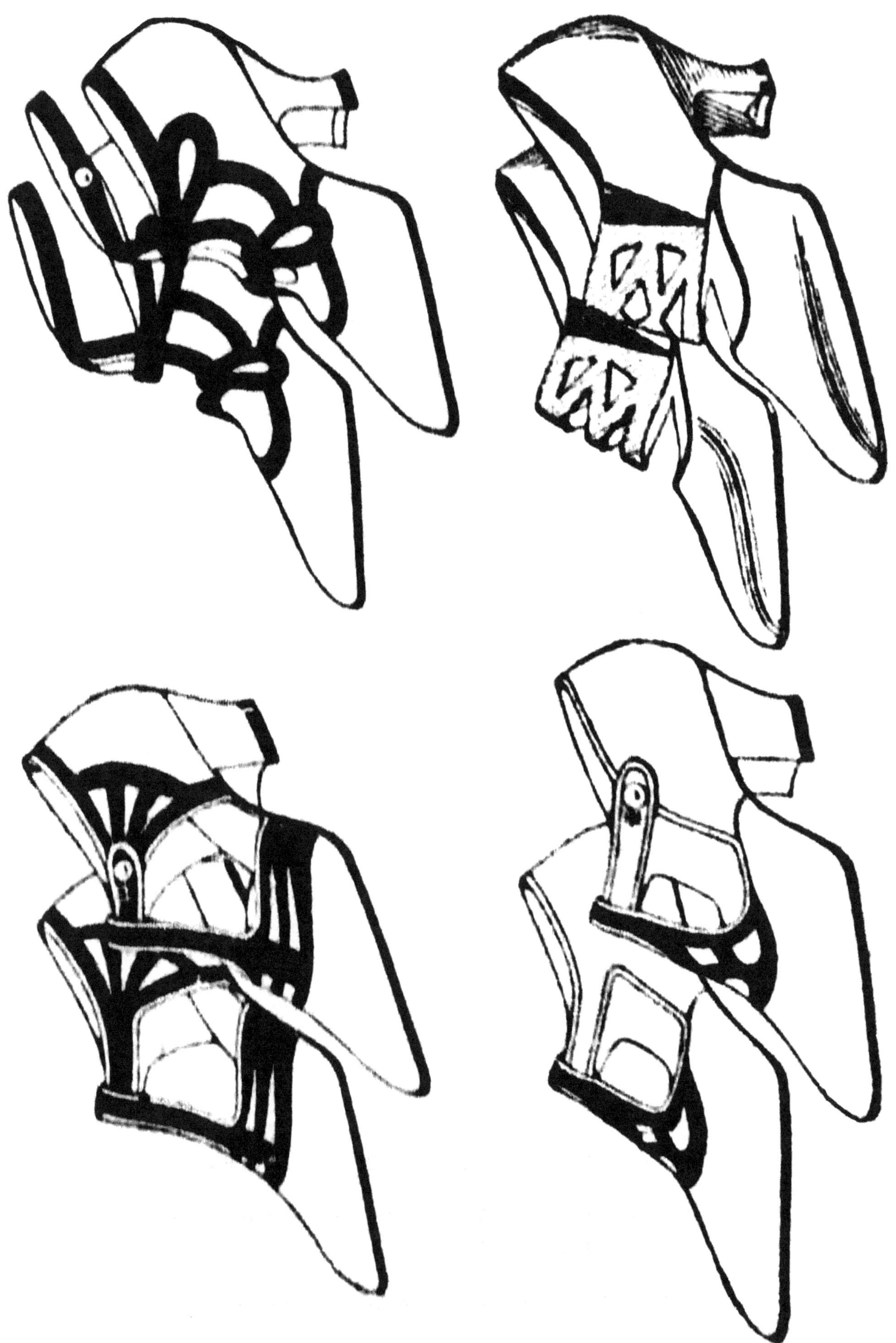

ABOUT THE ILLUSTRATION ON THE REVERSE

Original publication: St Louis Star and Times (Missouri)
Publication date: December 5, 1923

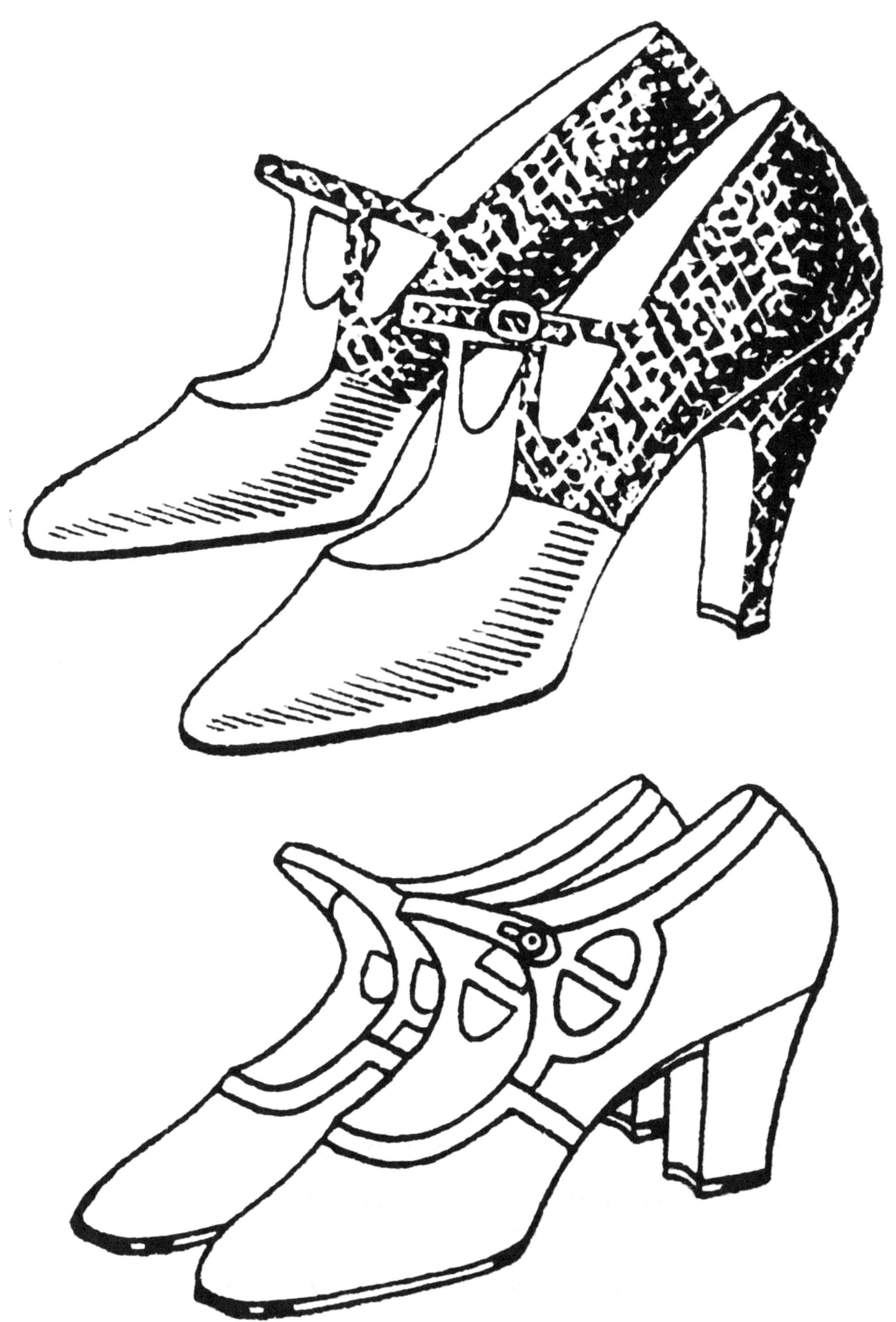

ABOUT THE ILLUSTRATION ON THE REVERSE

Original publication: El Paso Evening Post (Texas)
Publication date: May 29, 1928

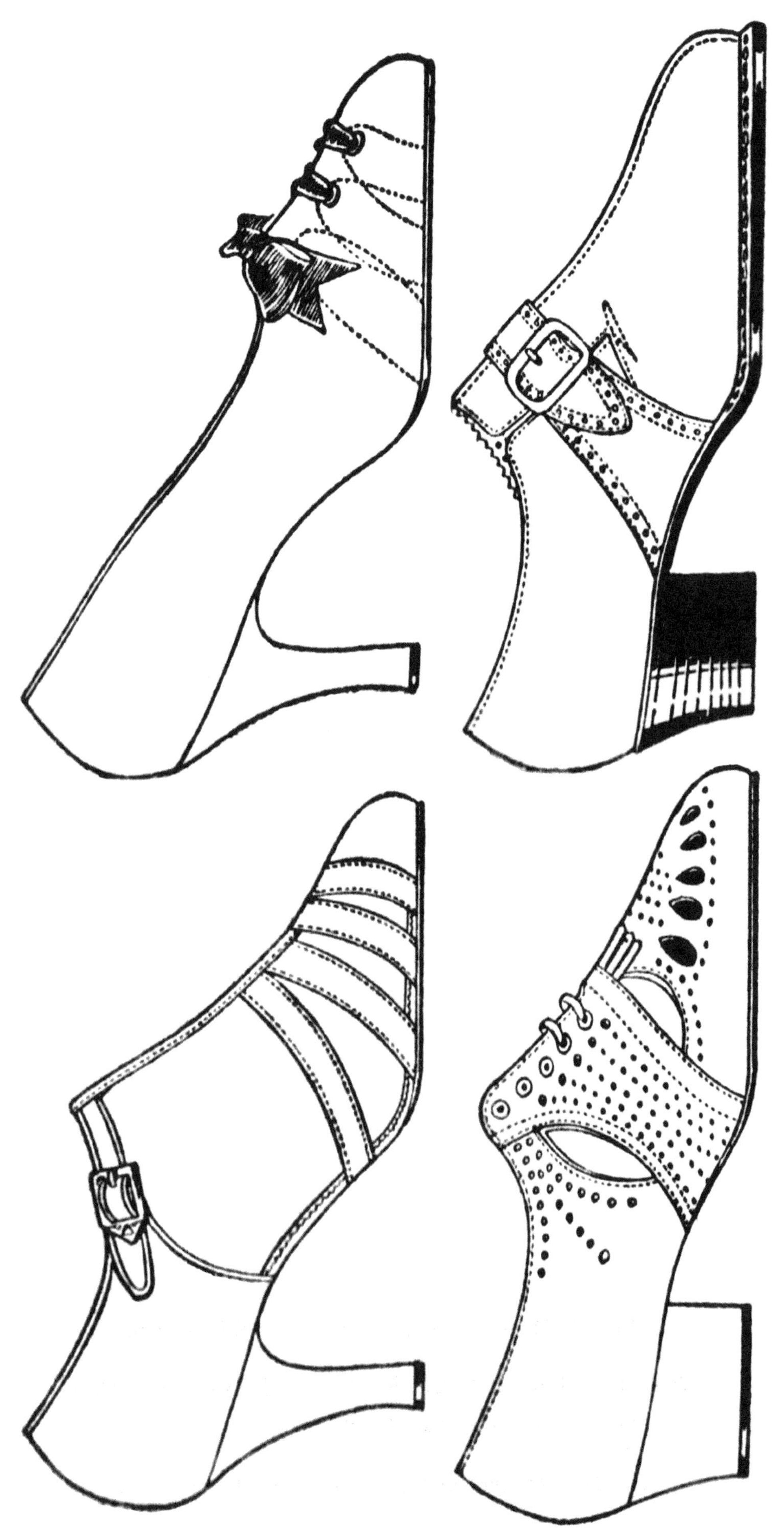

ABOUT THE ILLUSTRATION ON THE REVERSE

Original publication: Clarion-Ledger (Jackson, Mississippi)
Publication date: July 10, 1935

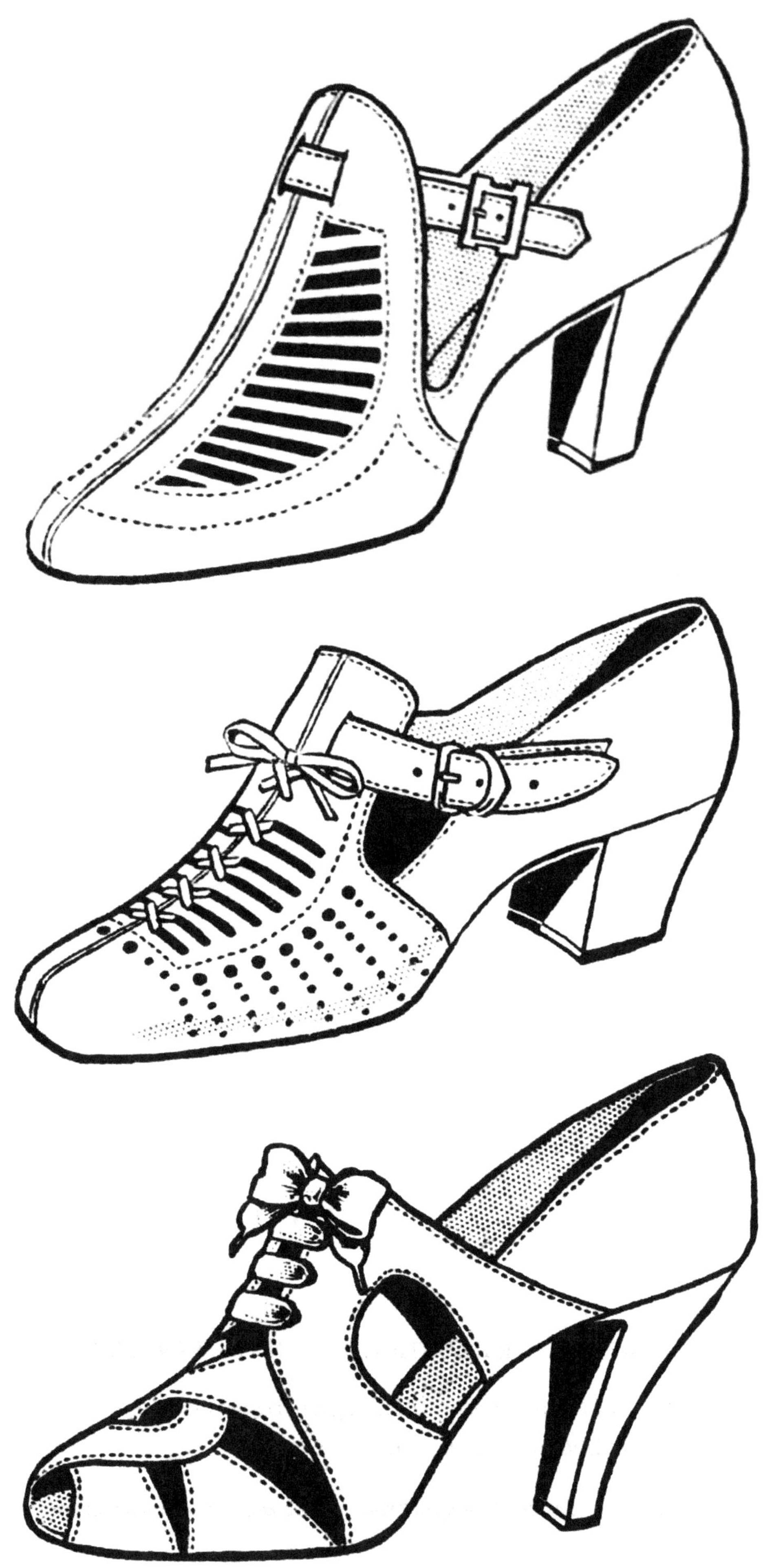

ABOUT THE ILLUSTRATION ON THE REVERSE

Original publication: Sheboygan Press (Wisconsin)
Publication date: June 8, 1937

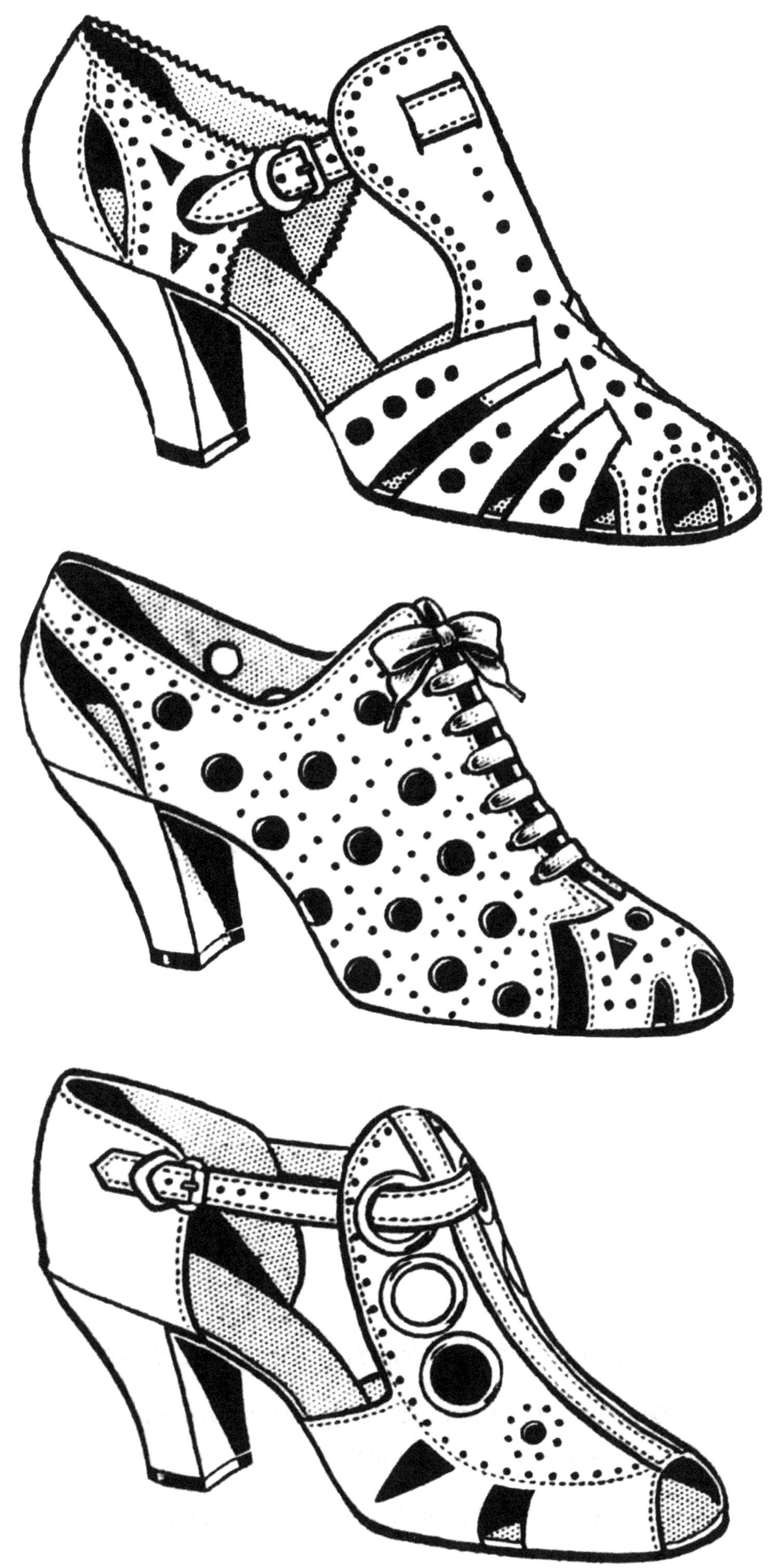

ABOUT THE ILLUSTRATION ON THE REVERSE

Original publication: Sheboygan Press (Wisconsin)
Publication date: June 8, 1937

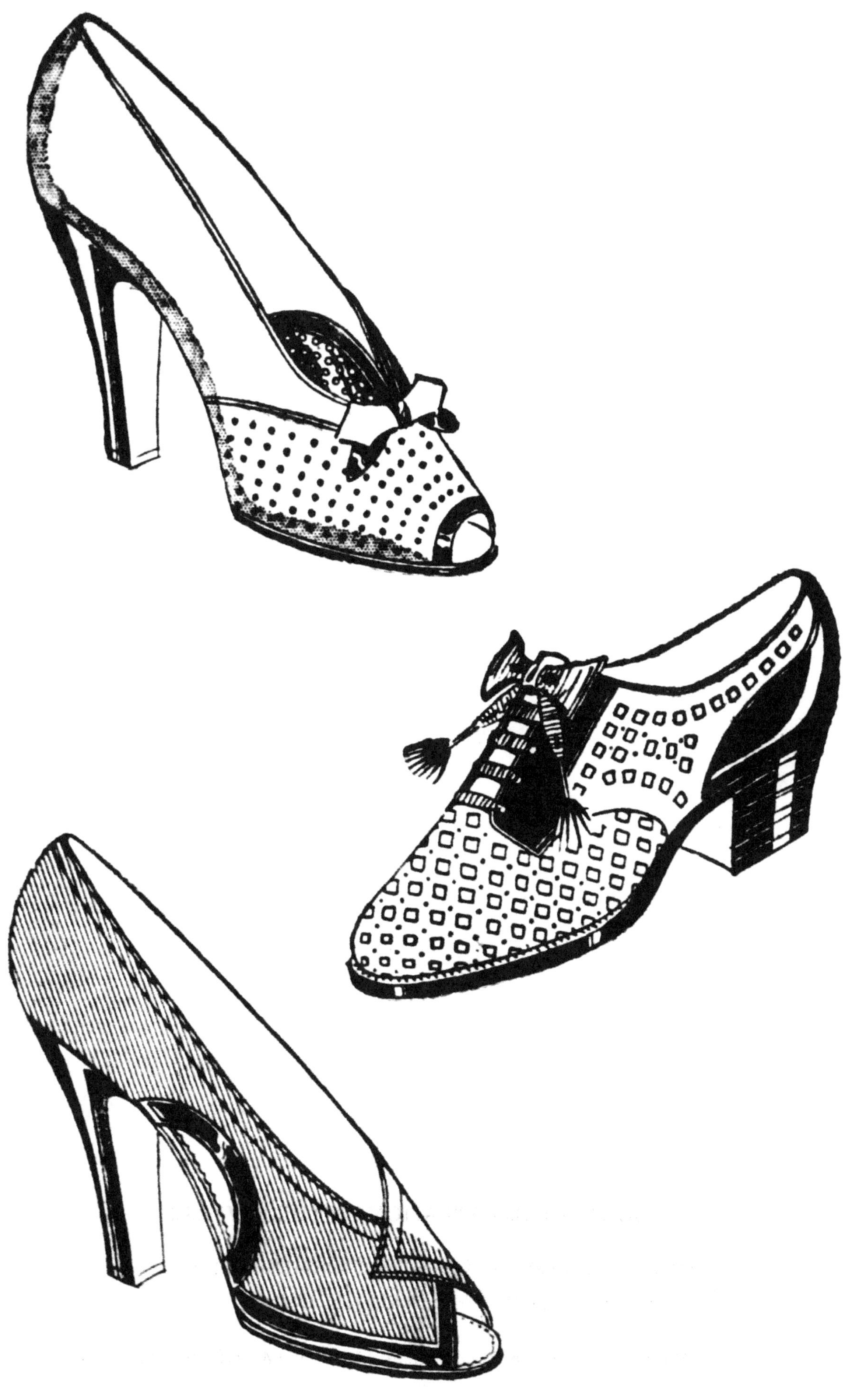

ABOUT THE ILLUSTRATION ON THE REVERSE

Original publication: Clarion Ledger (Mississippi)
Publication date: March 4, 1938

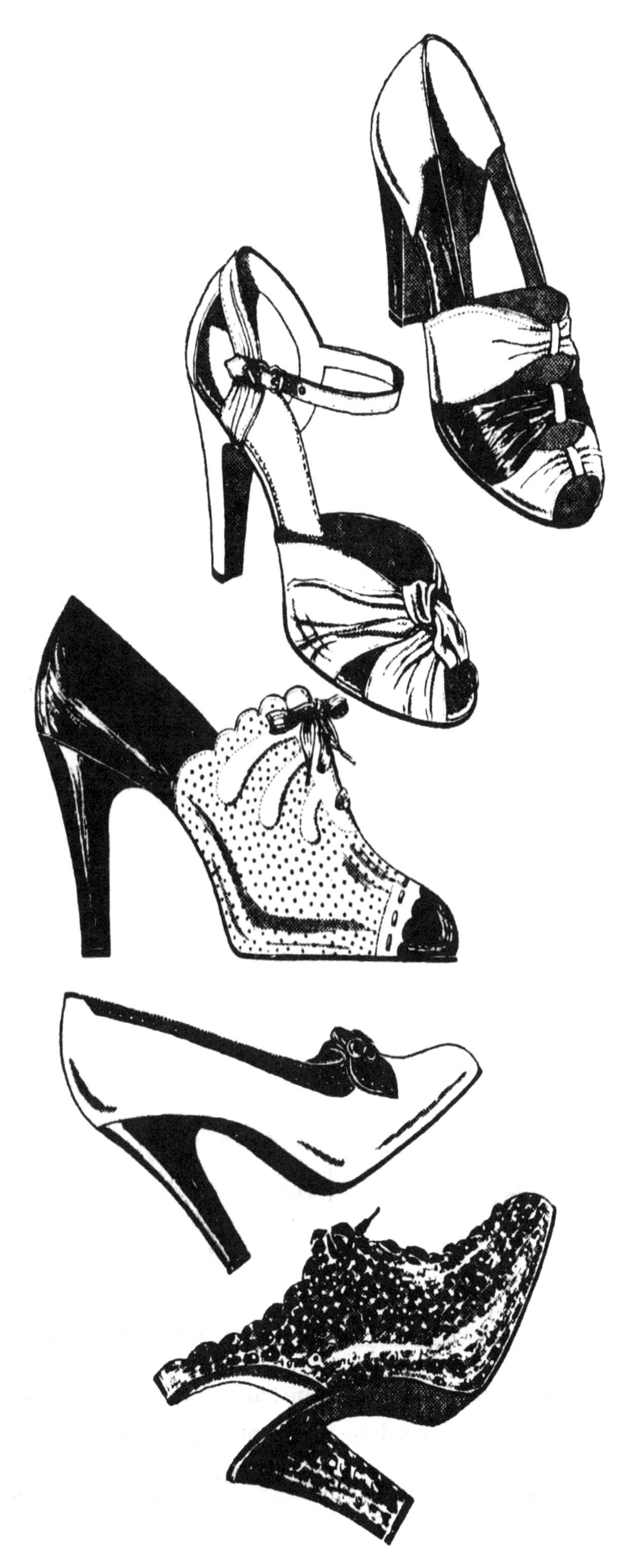

ABOUT THE ILLUSTRATION ON THE REVERSE

Original publication: The Palm Beach Post (Florida)
Publication date: November 13, 1938

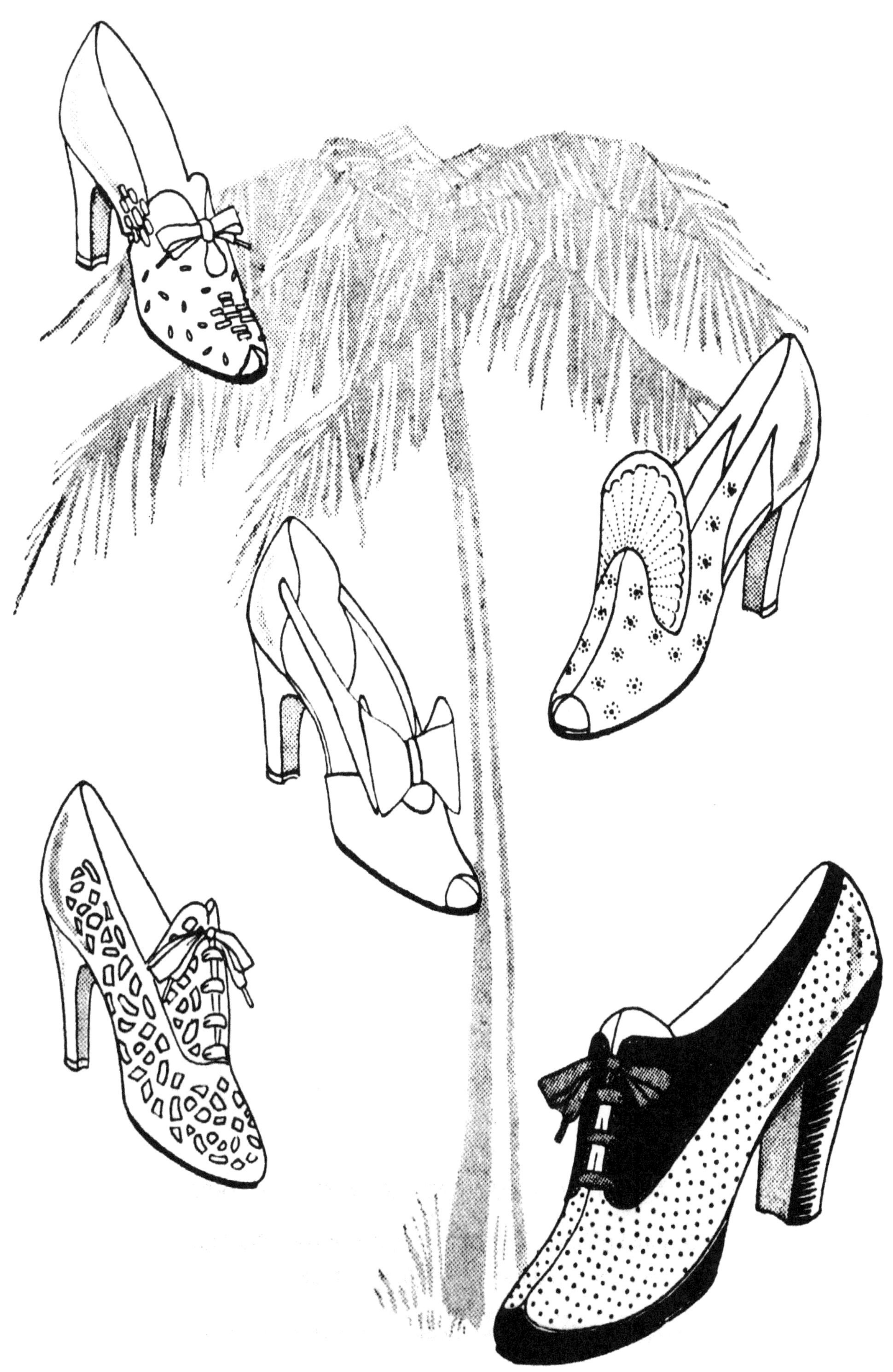

ABOUT THE ILLUSTRATION ON THE REVERSE

Original publication: The Palm Beach Post (Florida)
Publication date: December 28, 1938

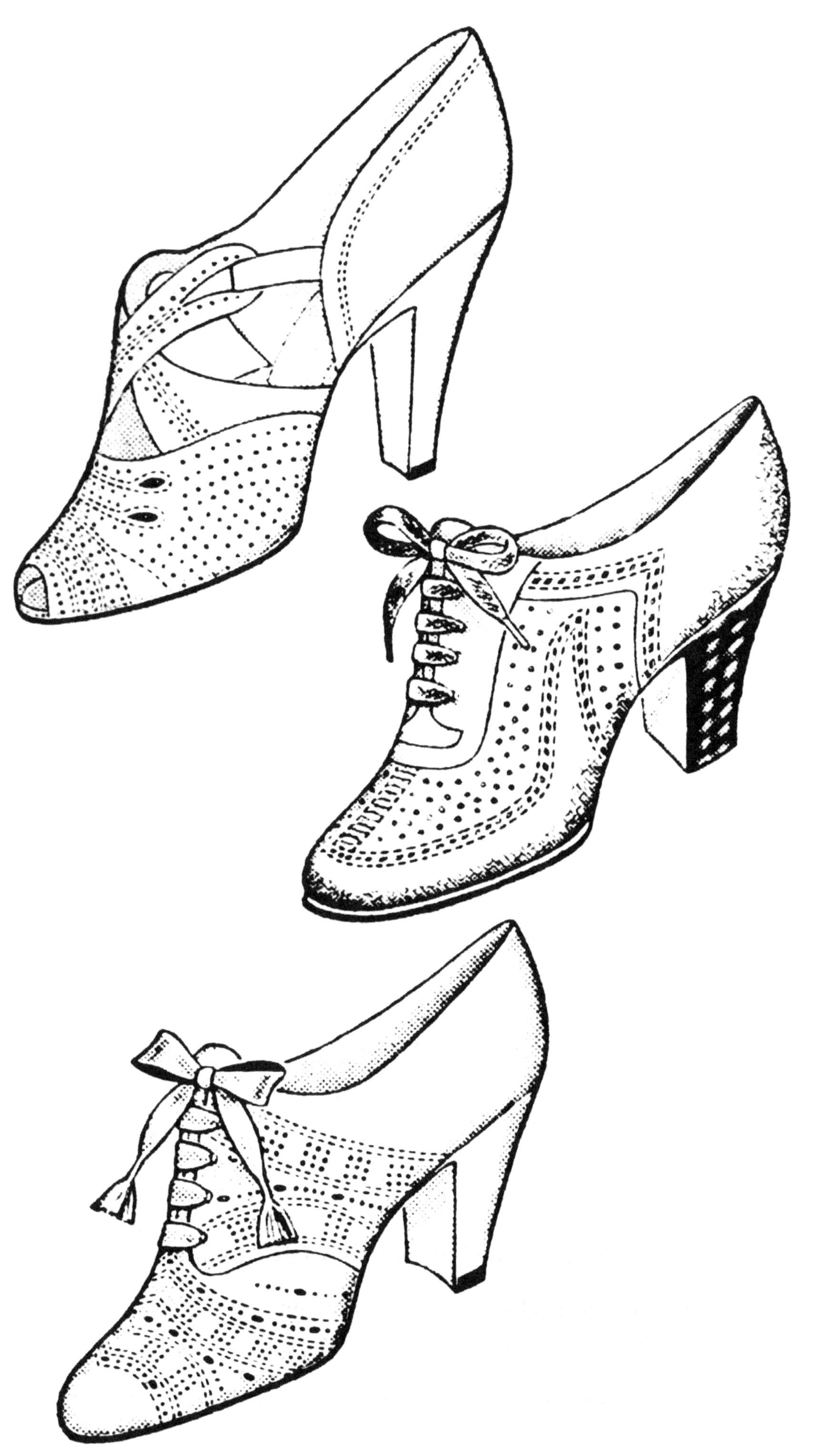

ABOUT THE ILLUSTRATION ON THE REVERSE

Original publication: St Louis Post Dispatch (MO)
Publication date: May 15, 1940

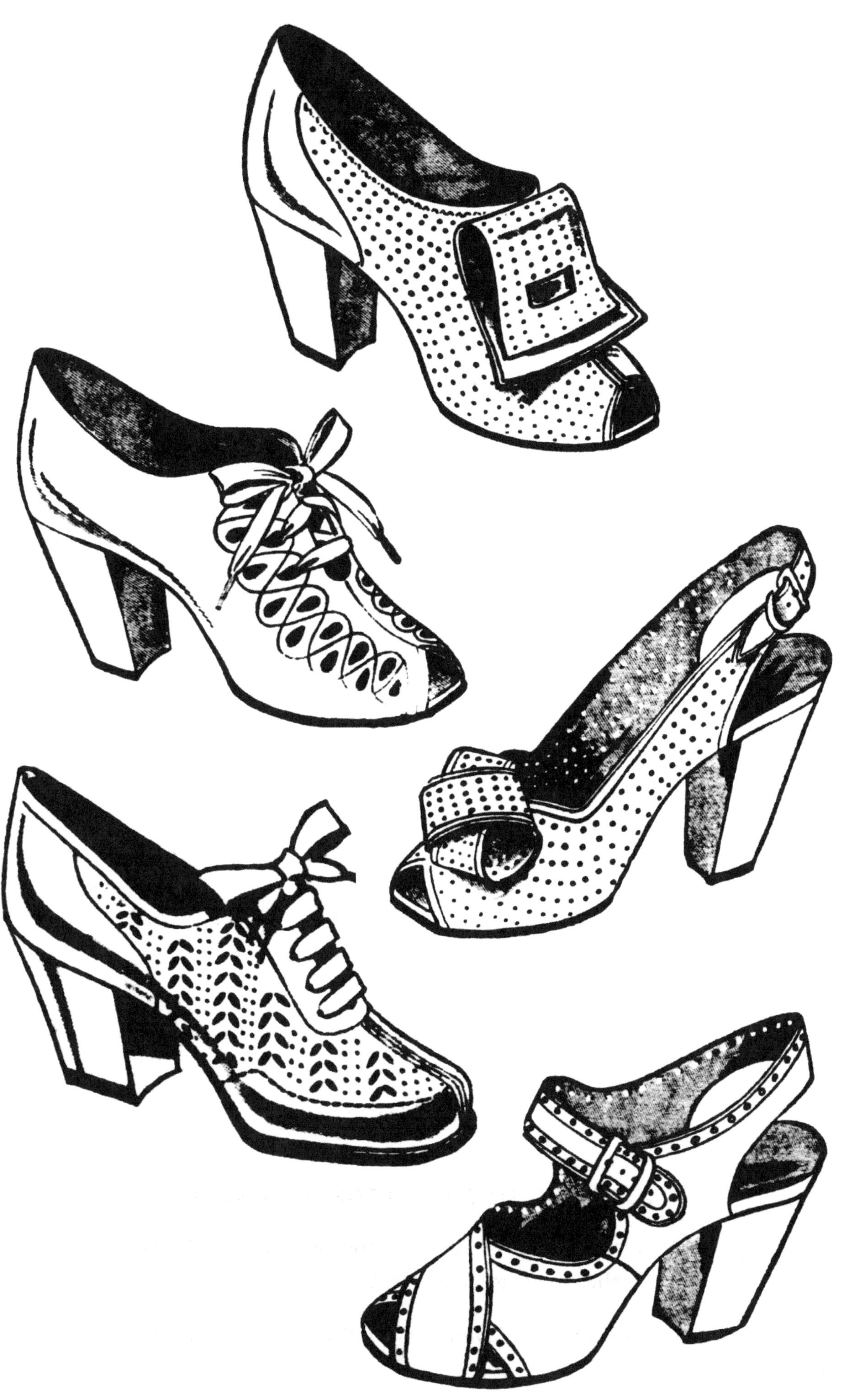

ABOUT THE ILLUSTRATION ON THE REVERSE

Original publication: Albuquerque Journal (New Mexico)
Publication date: May 7, 1948

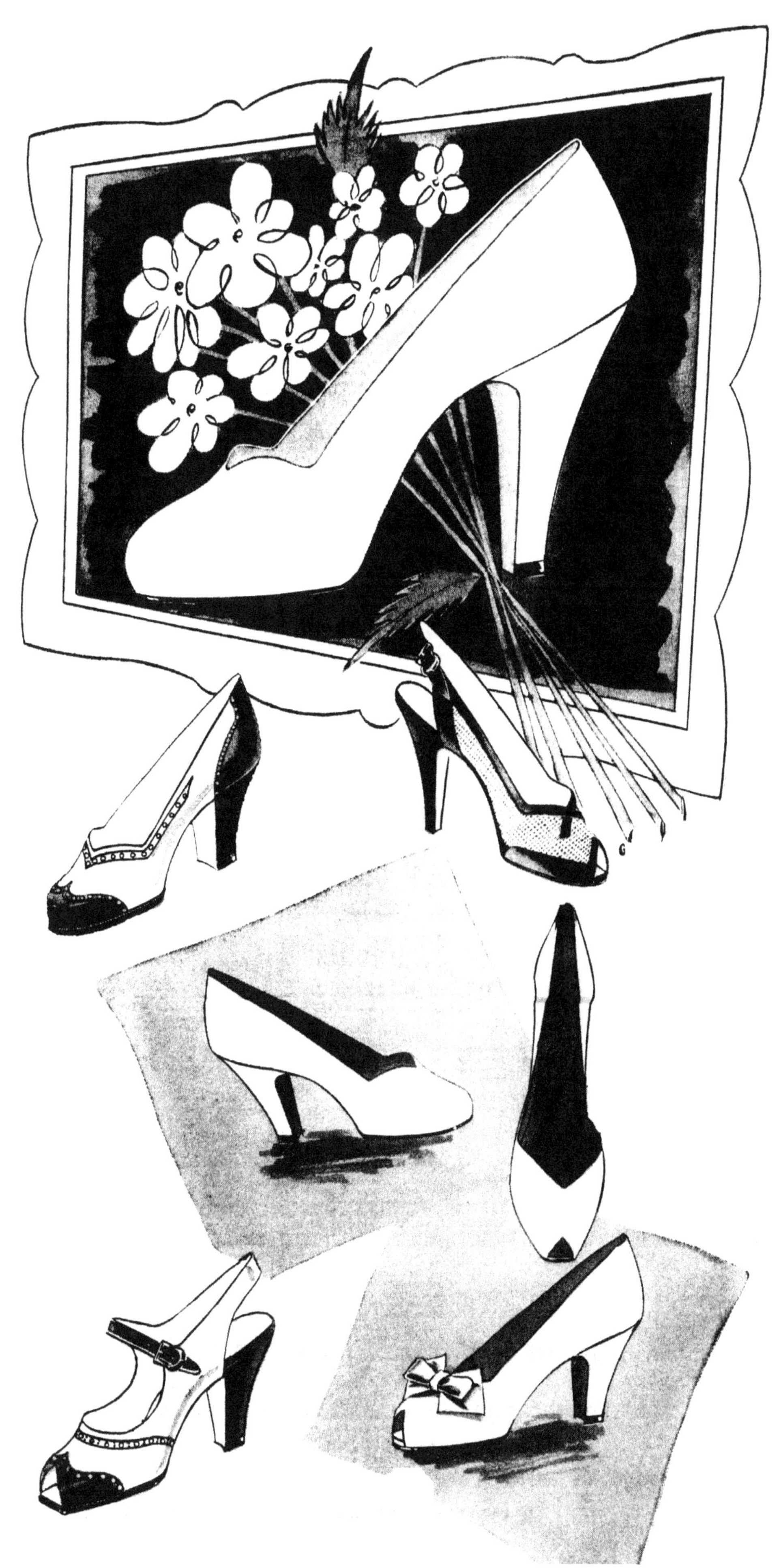

ABOUT THE ILLUSTRATION ON THE REVERSE

Original publication: Cincinnati Enquirer (Ohio)
Publication date: May 3, 1951

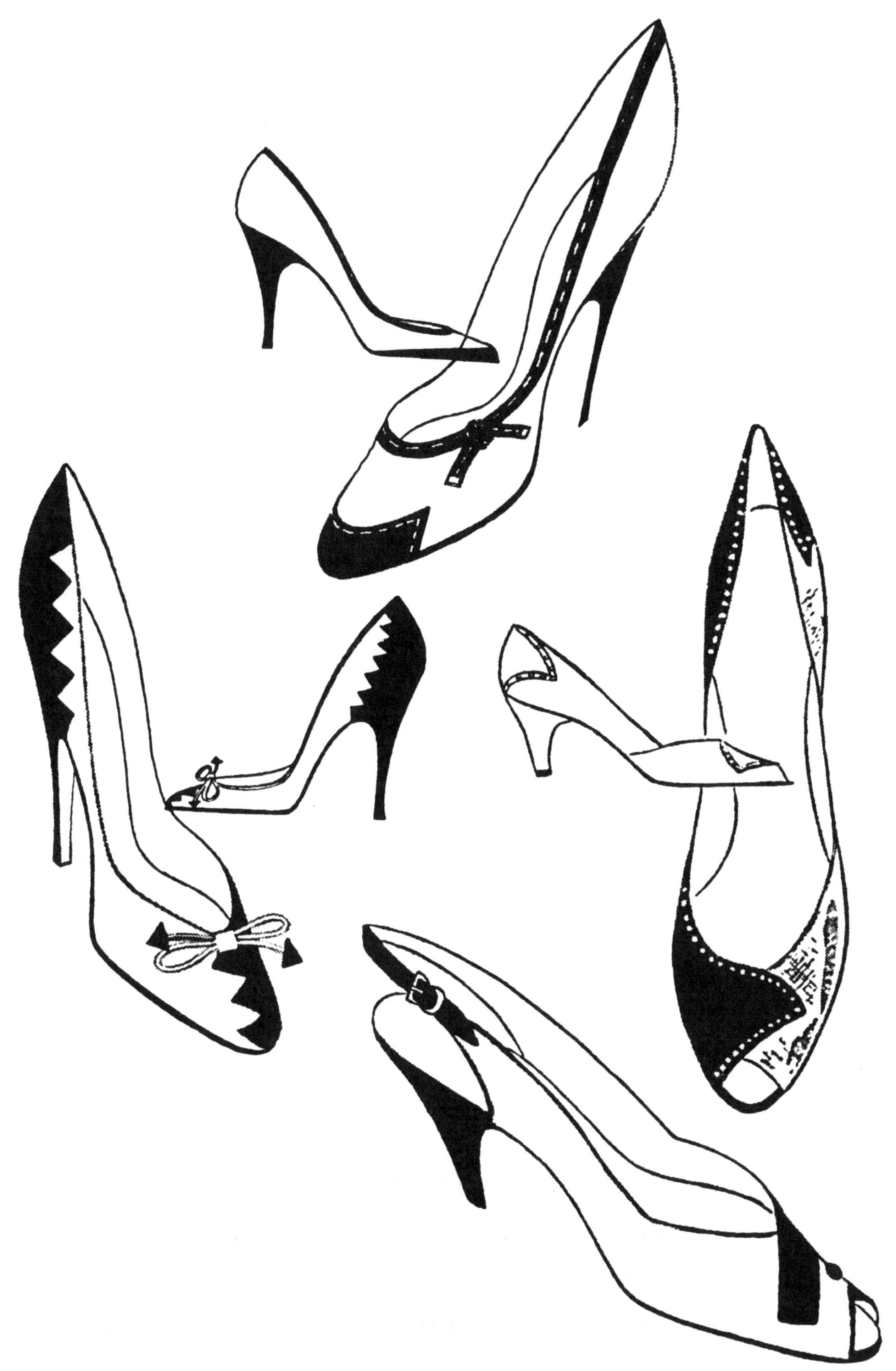

ABOUT THE ILLUSTRATION ON THE REVERSE

Original publication: Clarion Ledger (Mississippi)
Publication date: March 7, 1954

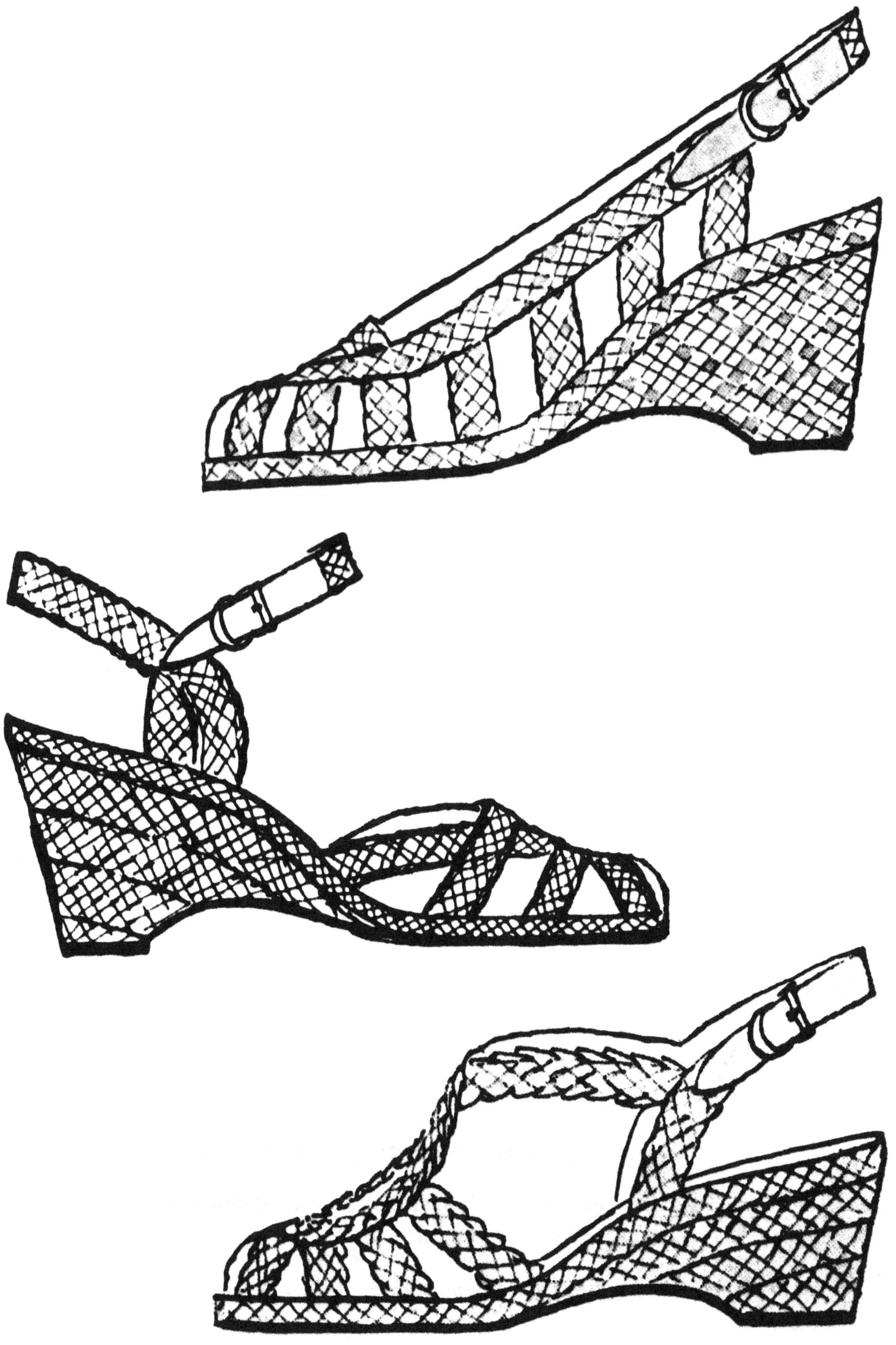

ABOUT THE ILLUSTRATION ON THE REVERSE

Original publication: Lincoln Star (Lincoln, Nebraska)

Publication date: March 31, 1954

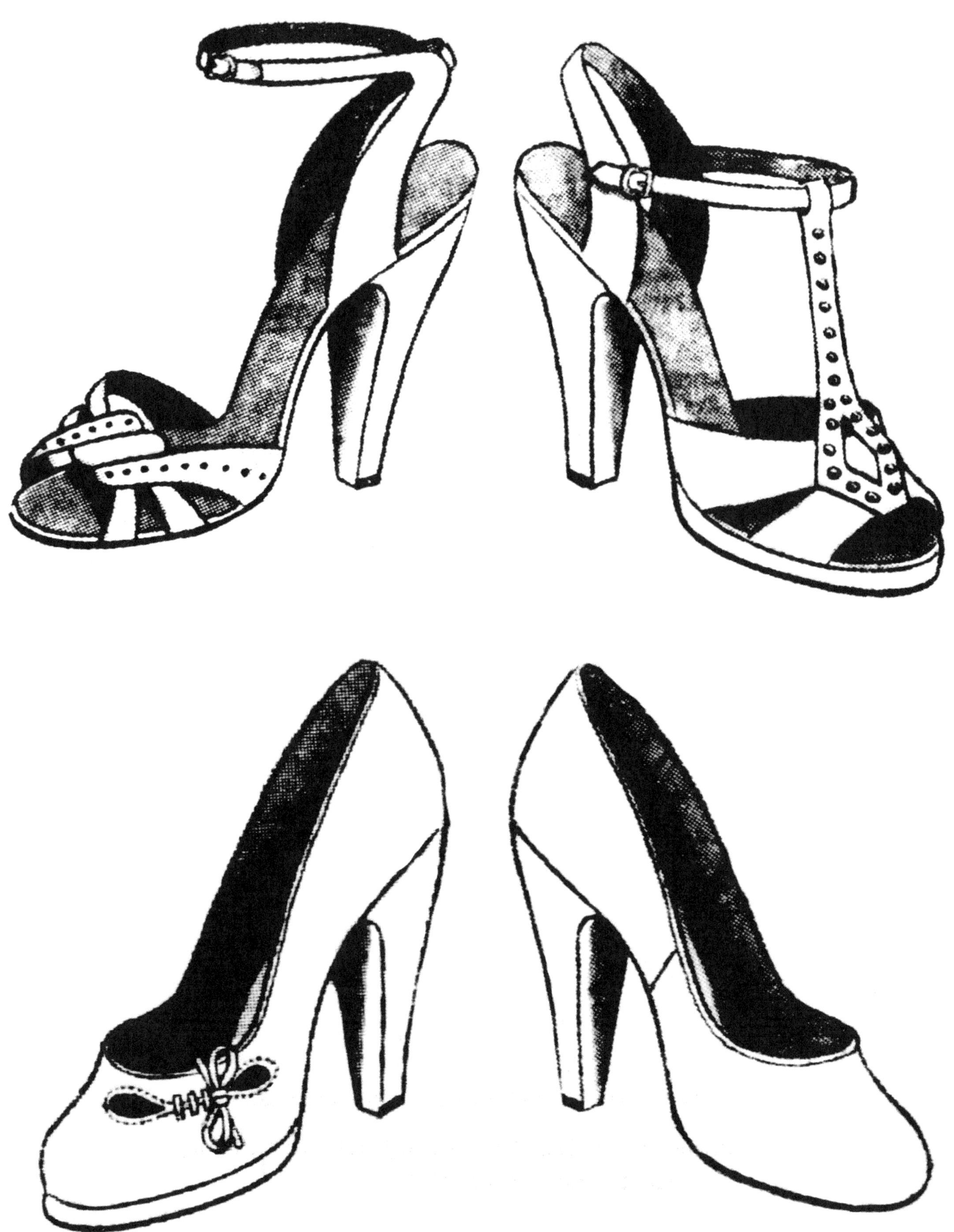

ABOUT THE ILLUSTRATION ON THE REVERSE

Original publication: Times Herald (Port Huron, Michigan)
Publication date: May 31, 1954

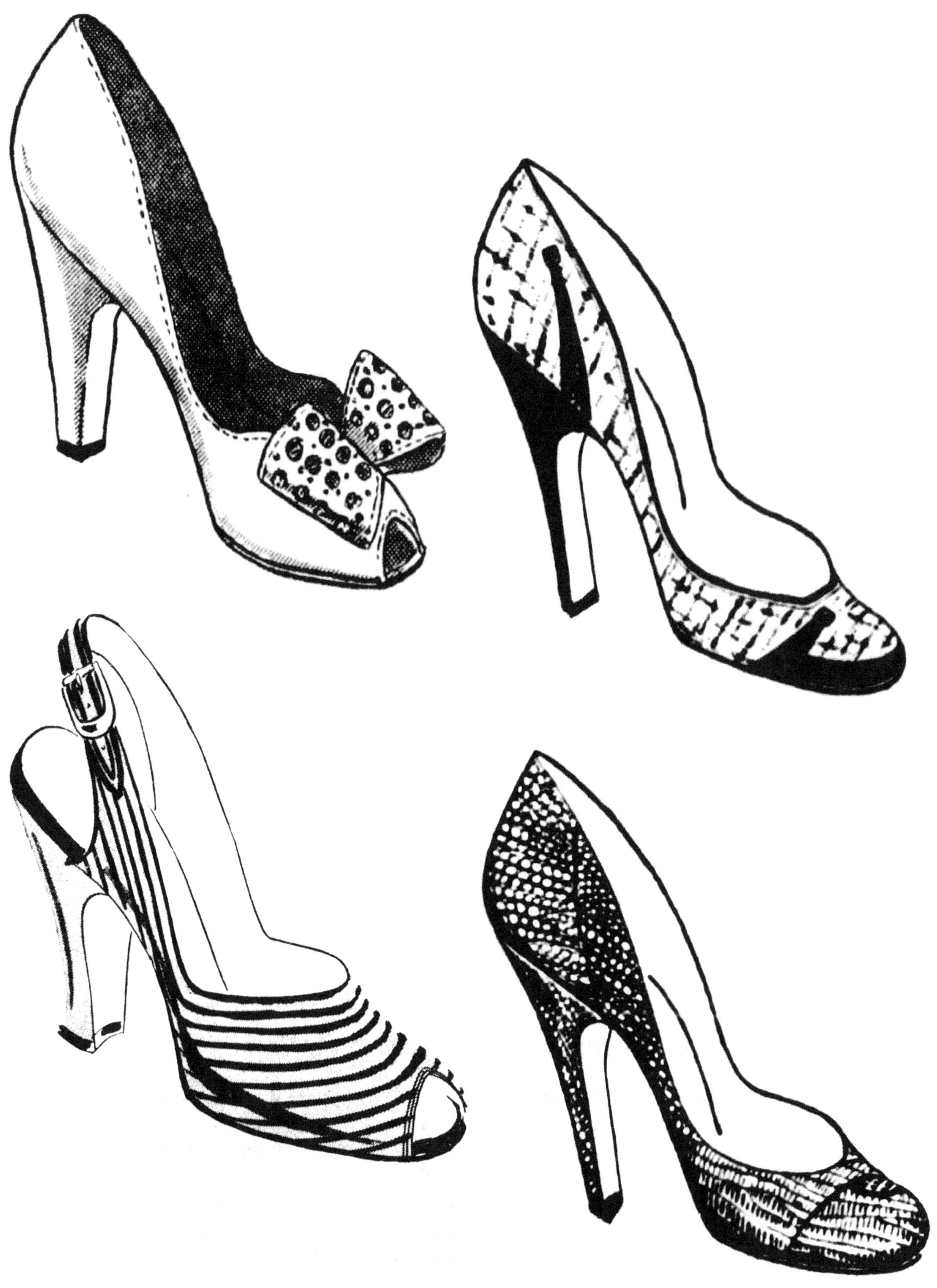

ABOUT THE ILLUSTRATION ON THE REVERSE

Original publication:	Clockwise from upper left: Palm Beach Post (Florida); Albuquerque Journal (New Mexico), Greenville News (South Carolina)
Publication date:	Clockwise from upper left: January 7, 1951; September 12, 1954; September 12, 1954; March 2, 1952

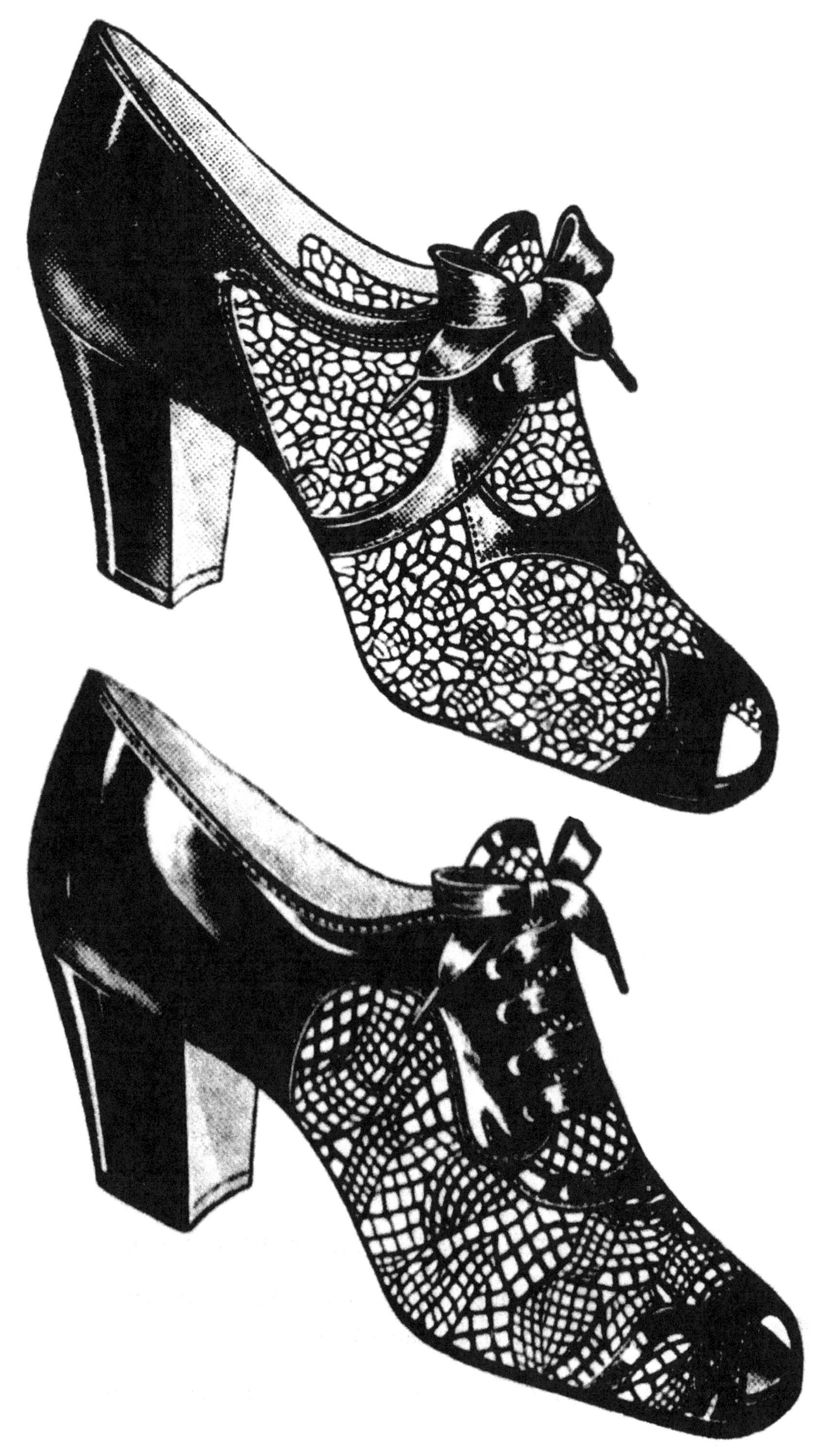

ABOUT THE ILLUSTRATION ON THE REVERSE

Original publication: Terre Haute Tribune (Indiana)
Publication date: March 3, 1957

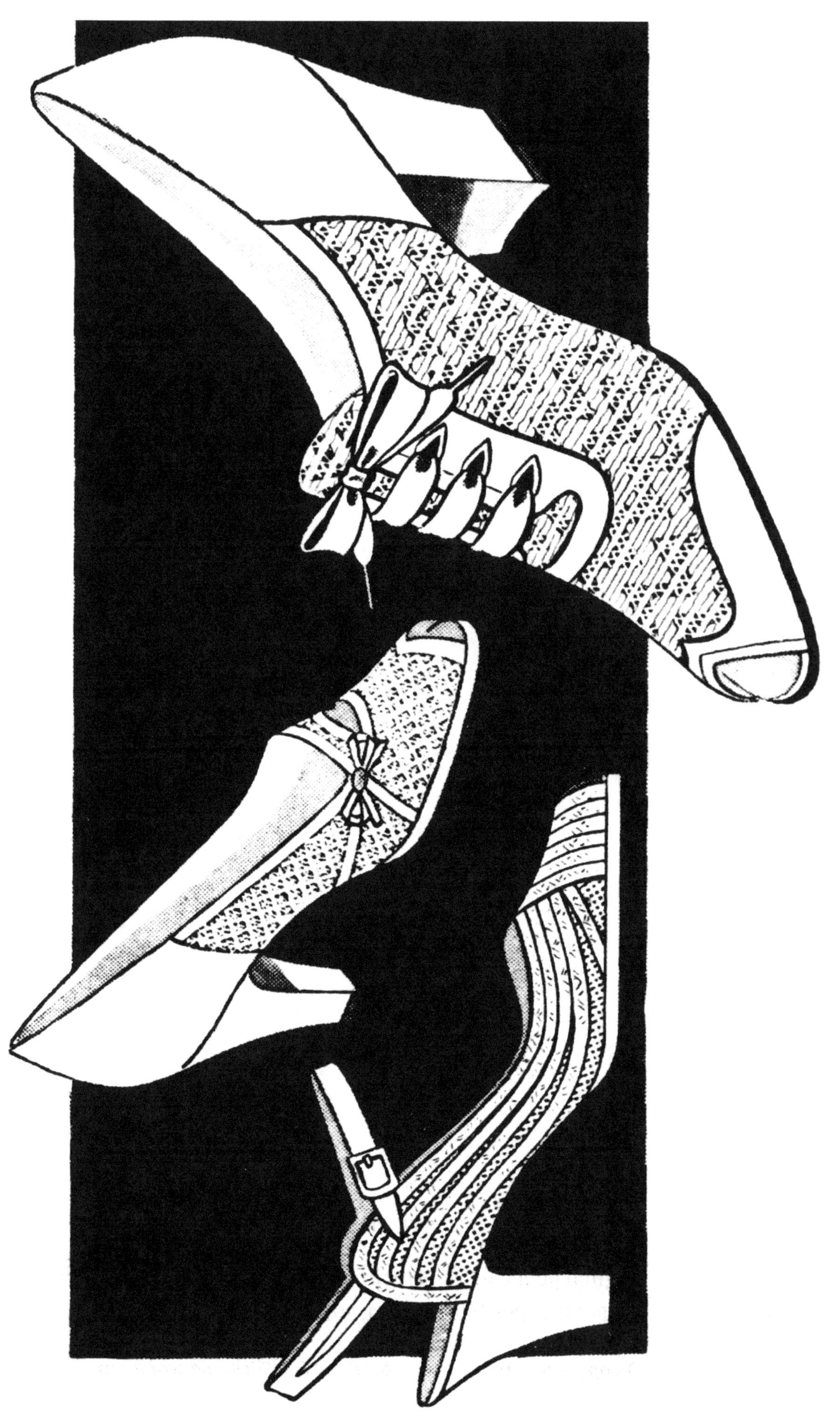

ABOUT THE ILLUSTRATION ON THE REVERSE

Original publication: Cincinnati Enquirer (Ohio)
Publication date: June 1, 1958

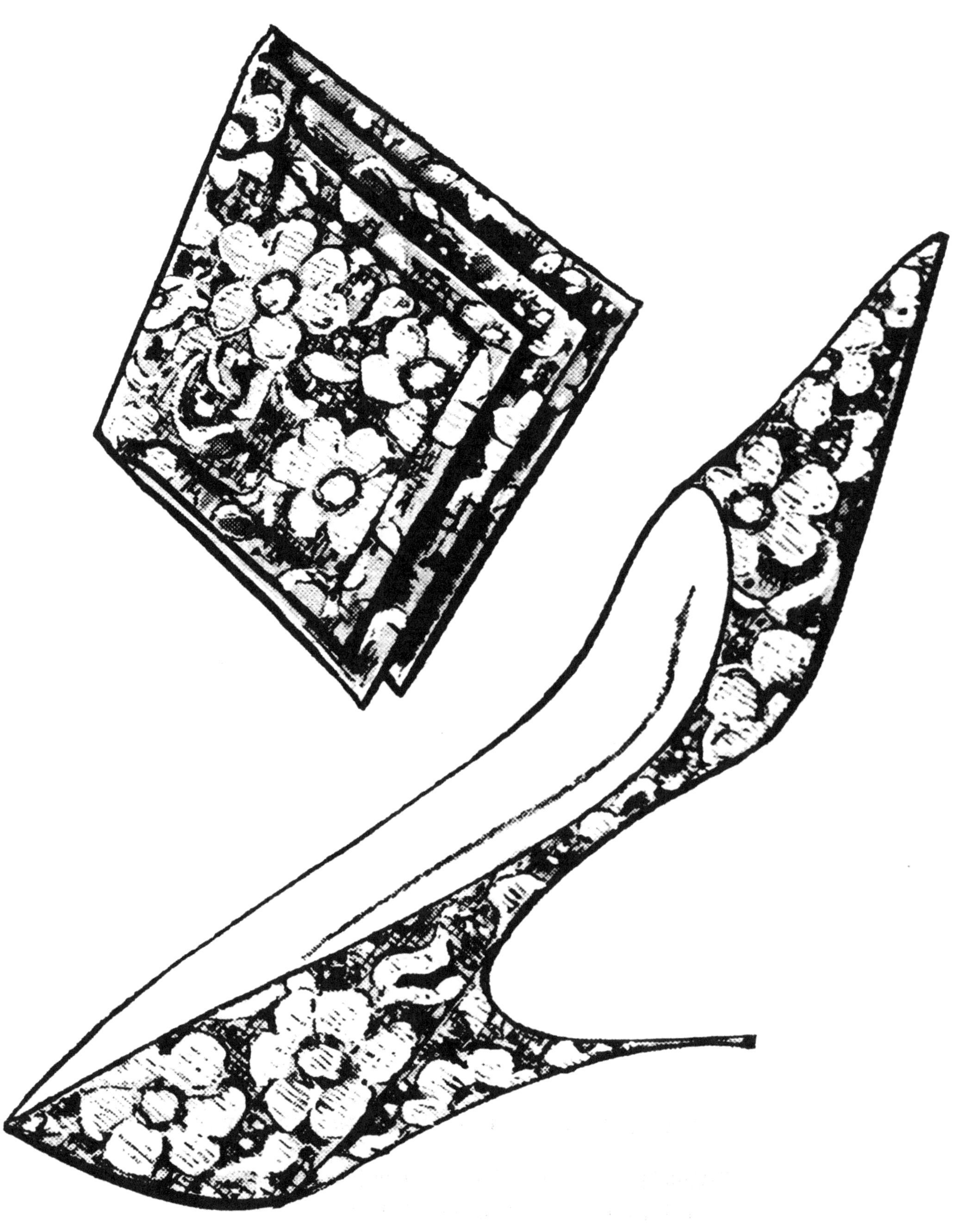

ABOUT THE ILLUSTRATION ON THE REVERSE

Original publication: Clarion Ledger (Mississippi)
Publication date: December 7, 1958

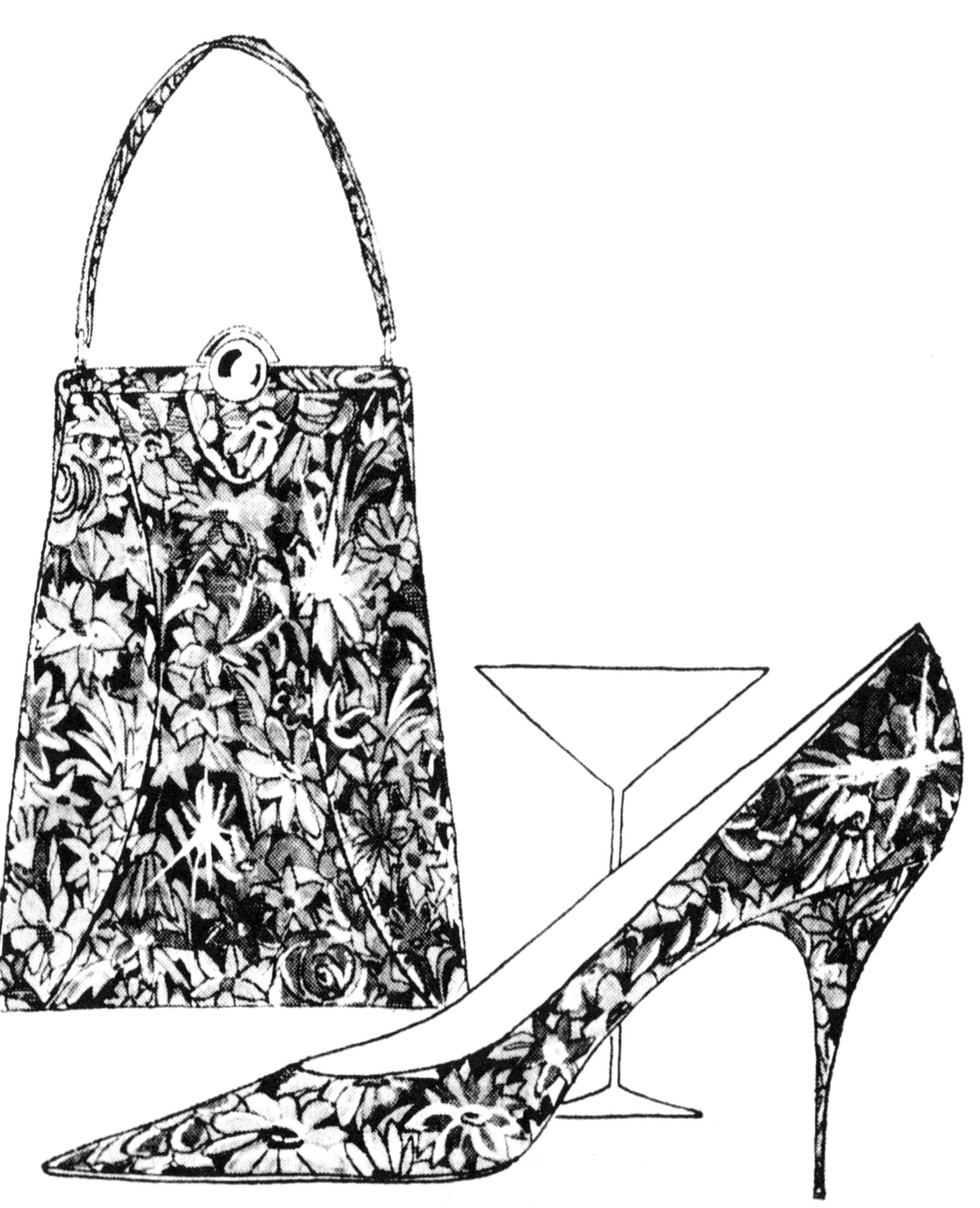

ABOUT THE ILLUSTRATION ON THE REVERSE

Original publication: Democrat and Chronicle (Rochester, NY)
Publication date: October 22, 1960

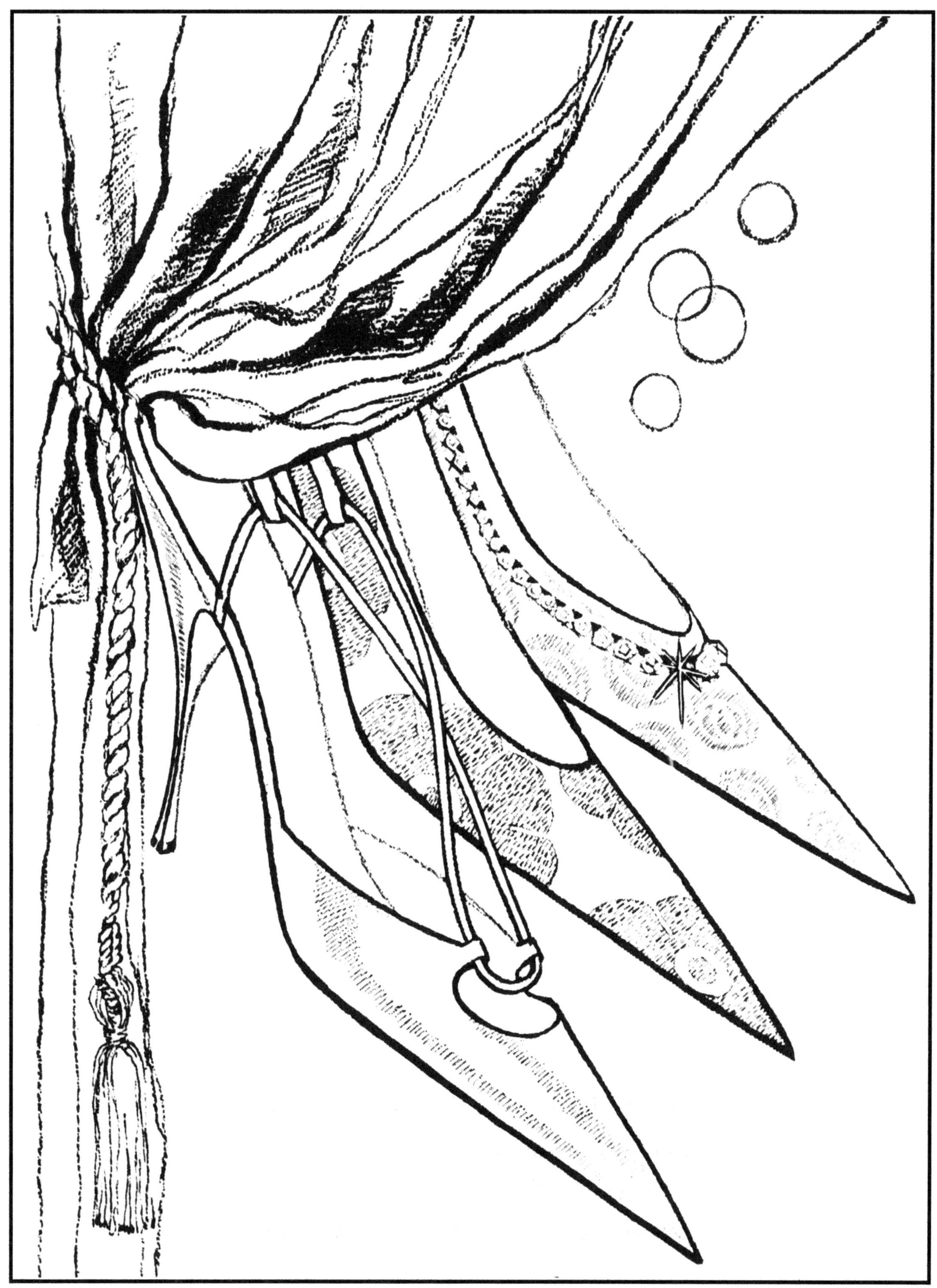

ABOUT THE ILLUSTRATION ON THE REVERSE

Original publication: Wisconsin Jewish Chronicle
Publication date: December 2, 1960

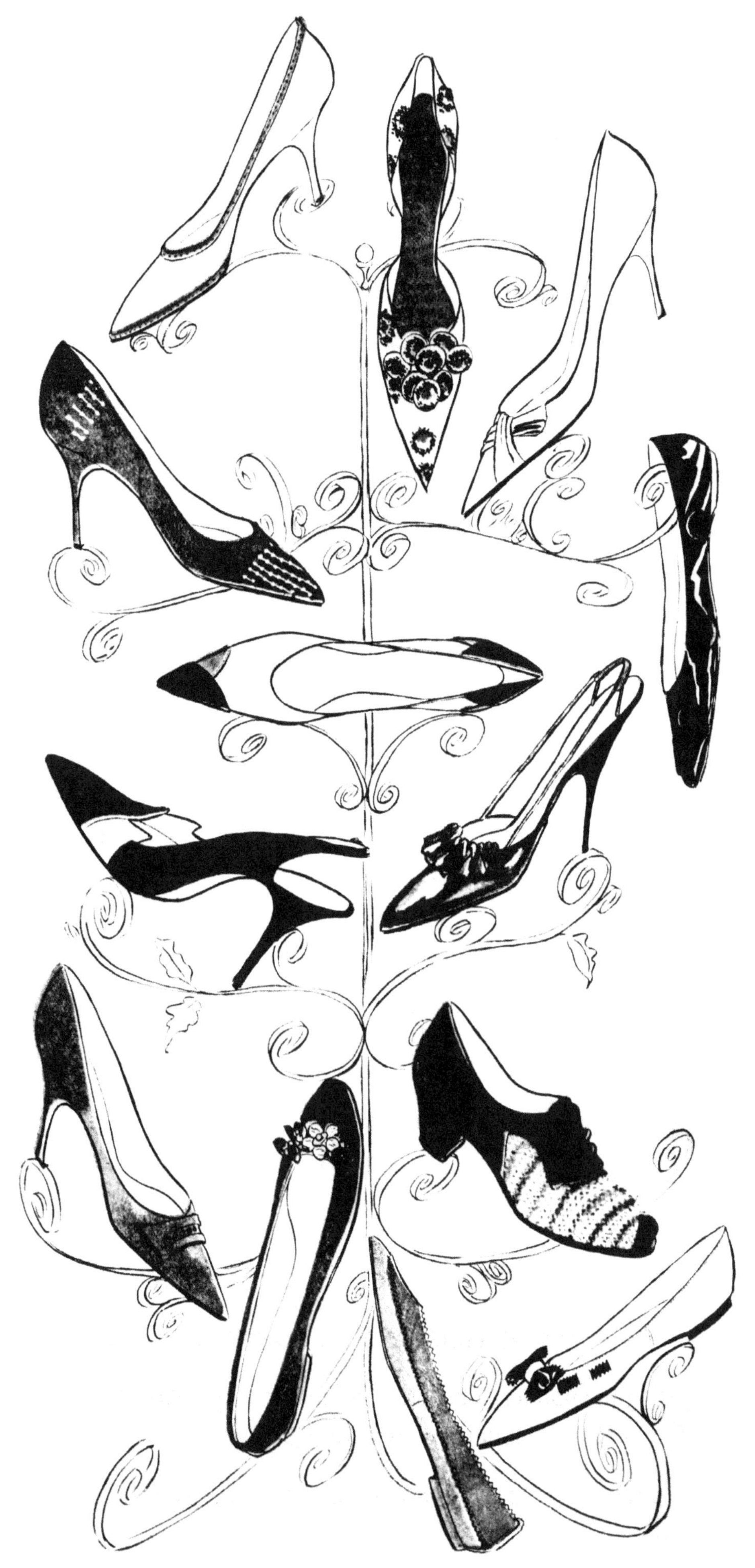

ABOUT THE ILLUSTRATION ON THE REVERSE

Original publication: The Orlando Sentinel (Florida)
Publication date: March 12, 1961

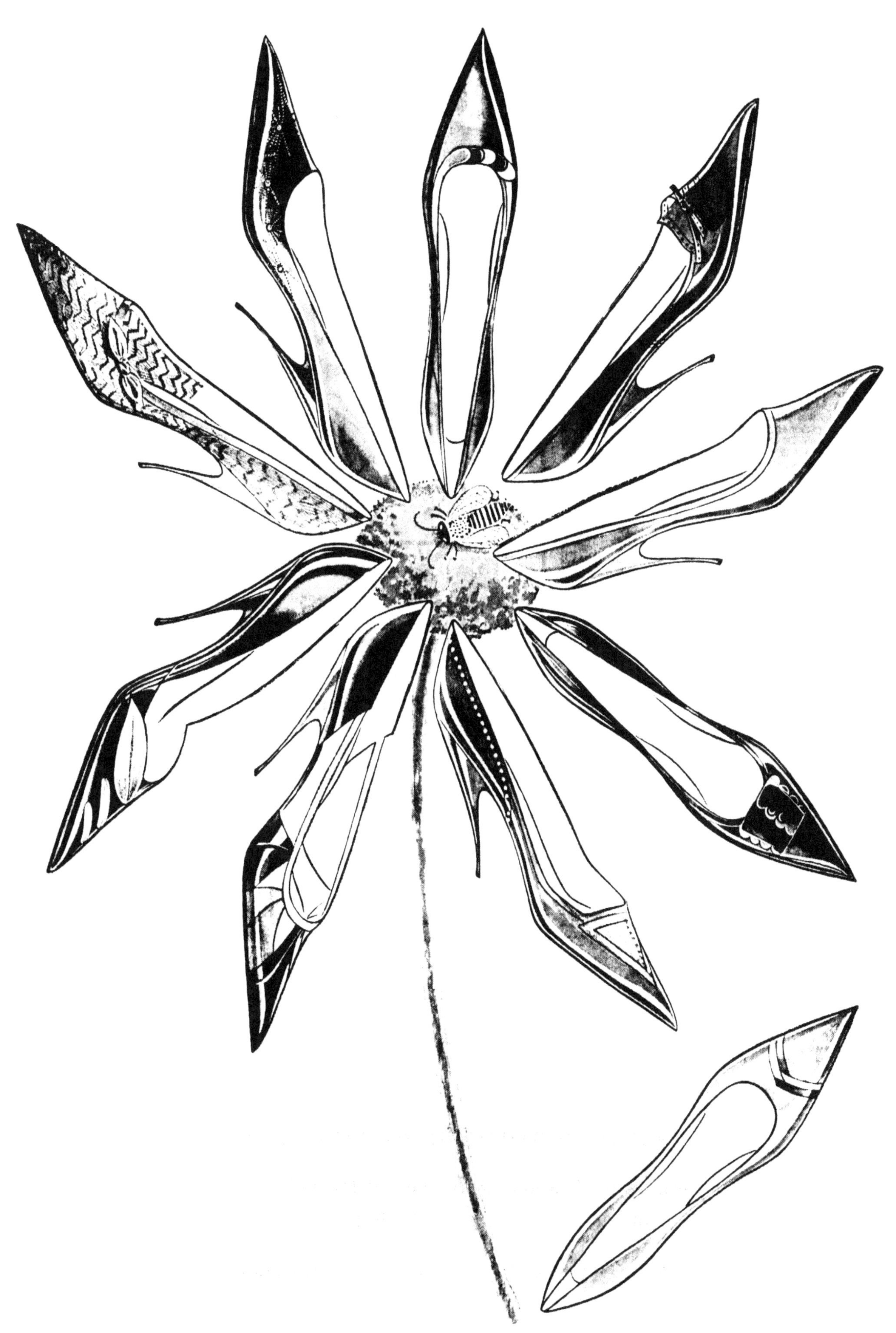

ABOUT THE ILLUSTRATION ON THE REVERSE

Original publication: Akron Beacon Journal (Ohio)
Publication date: March 23, 1961

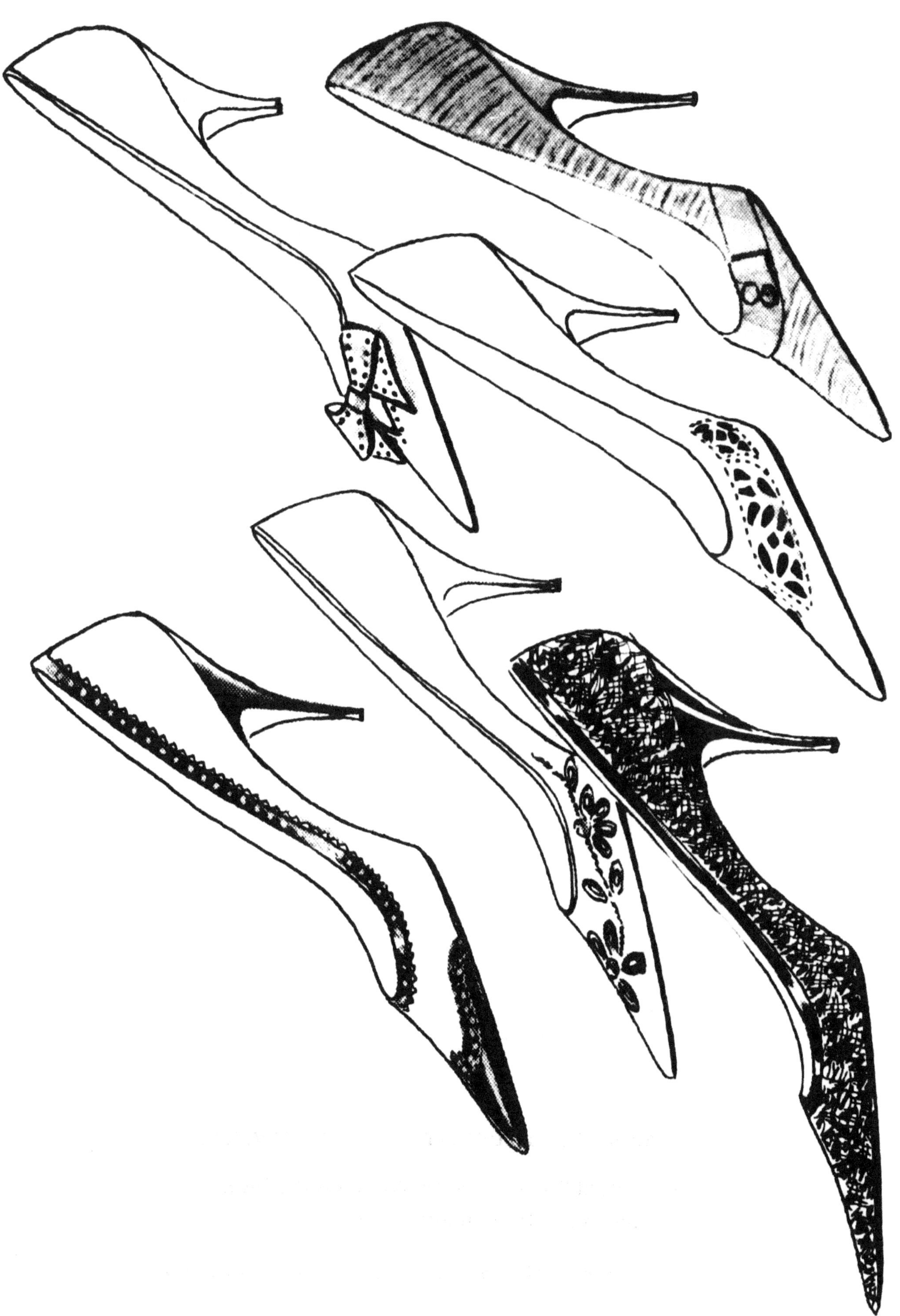

ABOUT THE ILLUSTRATION ON THE REVERSE

Original publication: Detroit Free Press (Michigan)
Publication date: June 29, 1961

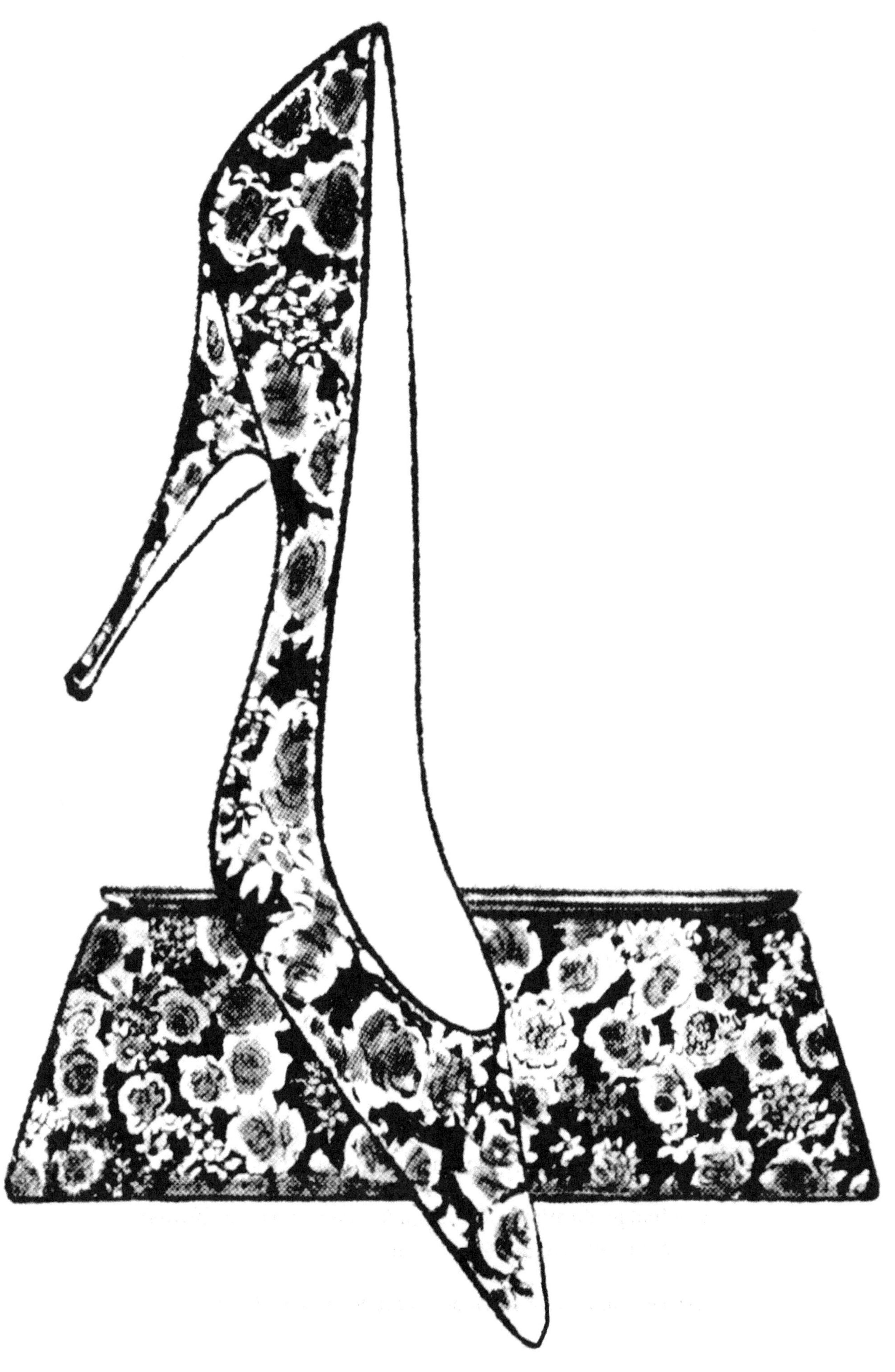

ABOUT THE ILLUSTRATION ON THE REVERSE

Original publication: Philadelphia Inquirer (Pennsylvania)
Publication date: May 23, 1962

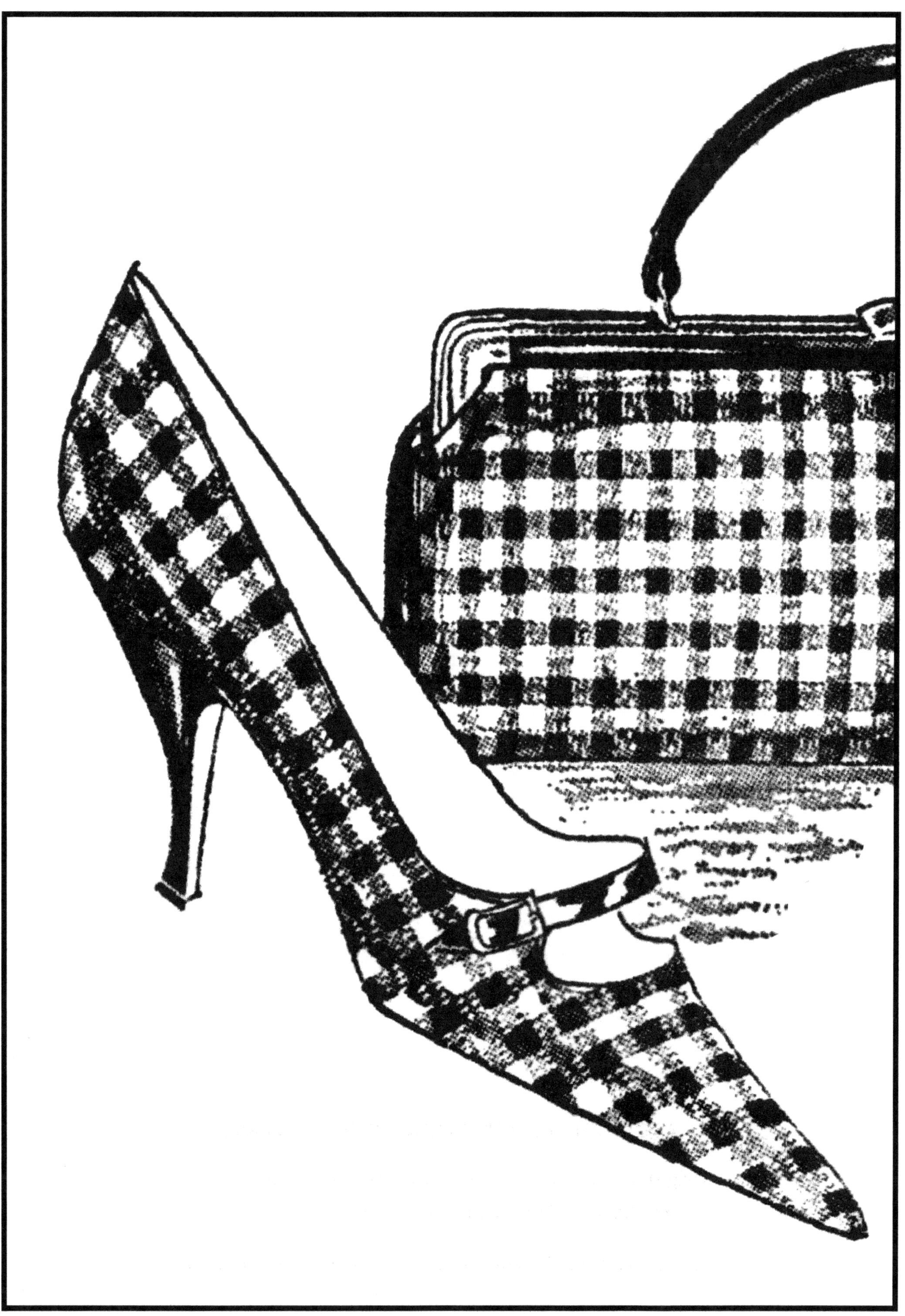

ABOUT THE ILLUSTRATION ON THE REVERSE

Original publication: Kansas City Times (Missouri)
Publication date: March 23, 1963

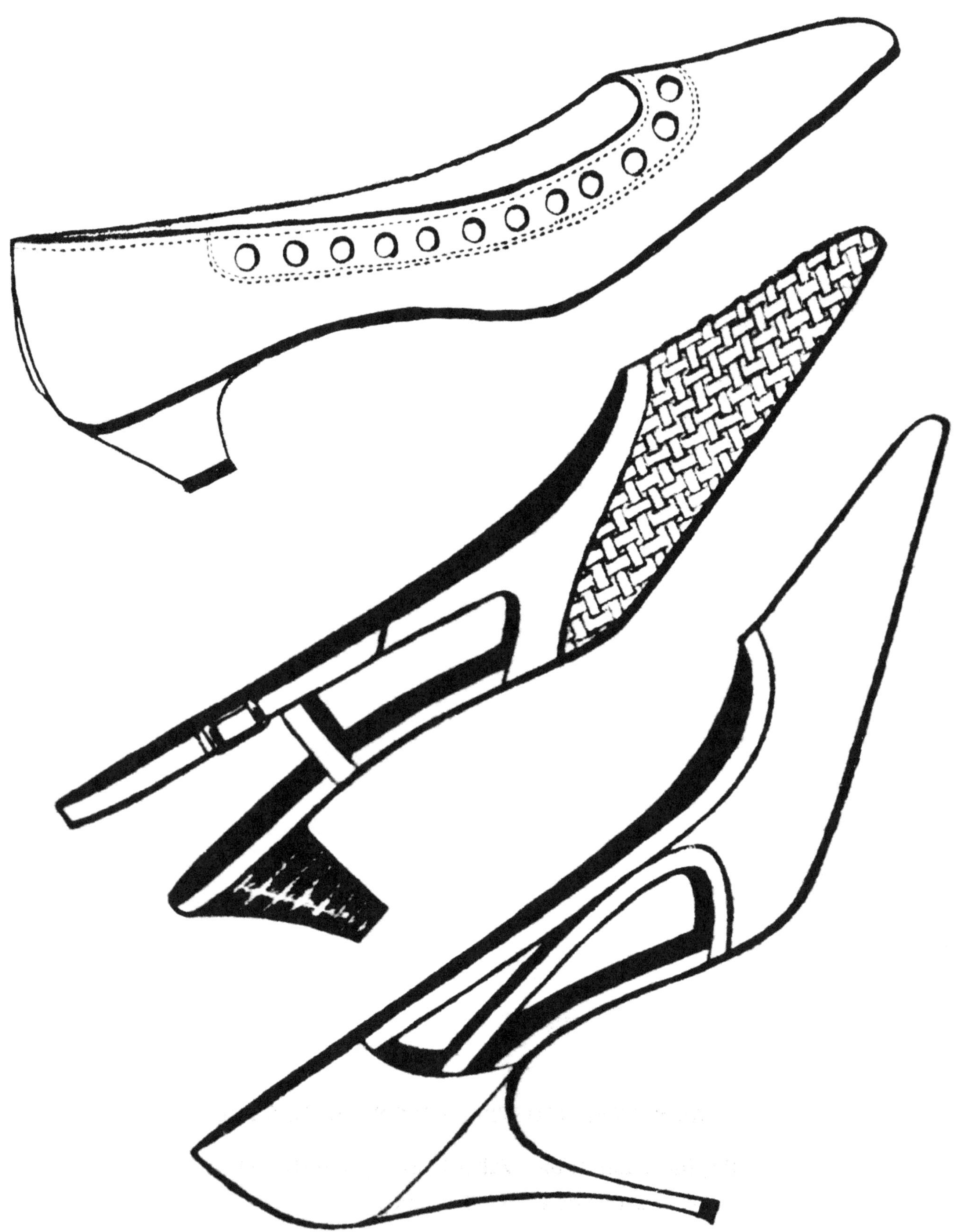

ABOUT THE ILLUSTRATION ON THE REVERSE

Original publication: Valley Morning Star (Texas)
Publication date: April 30, 1965

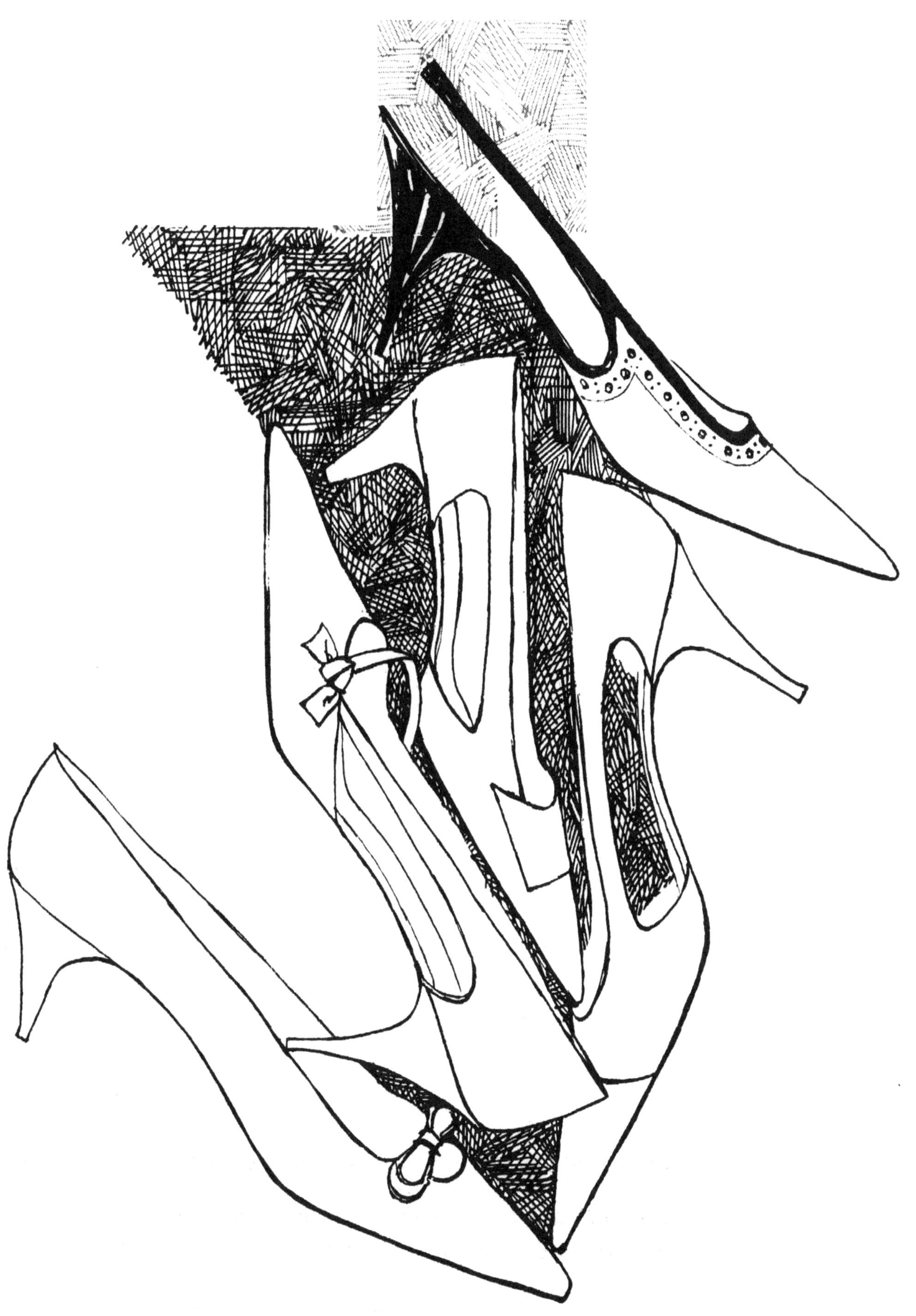

ABOUT THE ILLUSTRATION ON THE REVERSE

Original publication: Pittsburgh Press (Pennsylvania)
Publication date: February 25, 1965

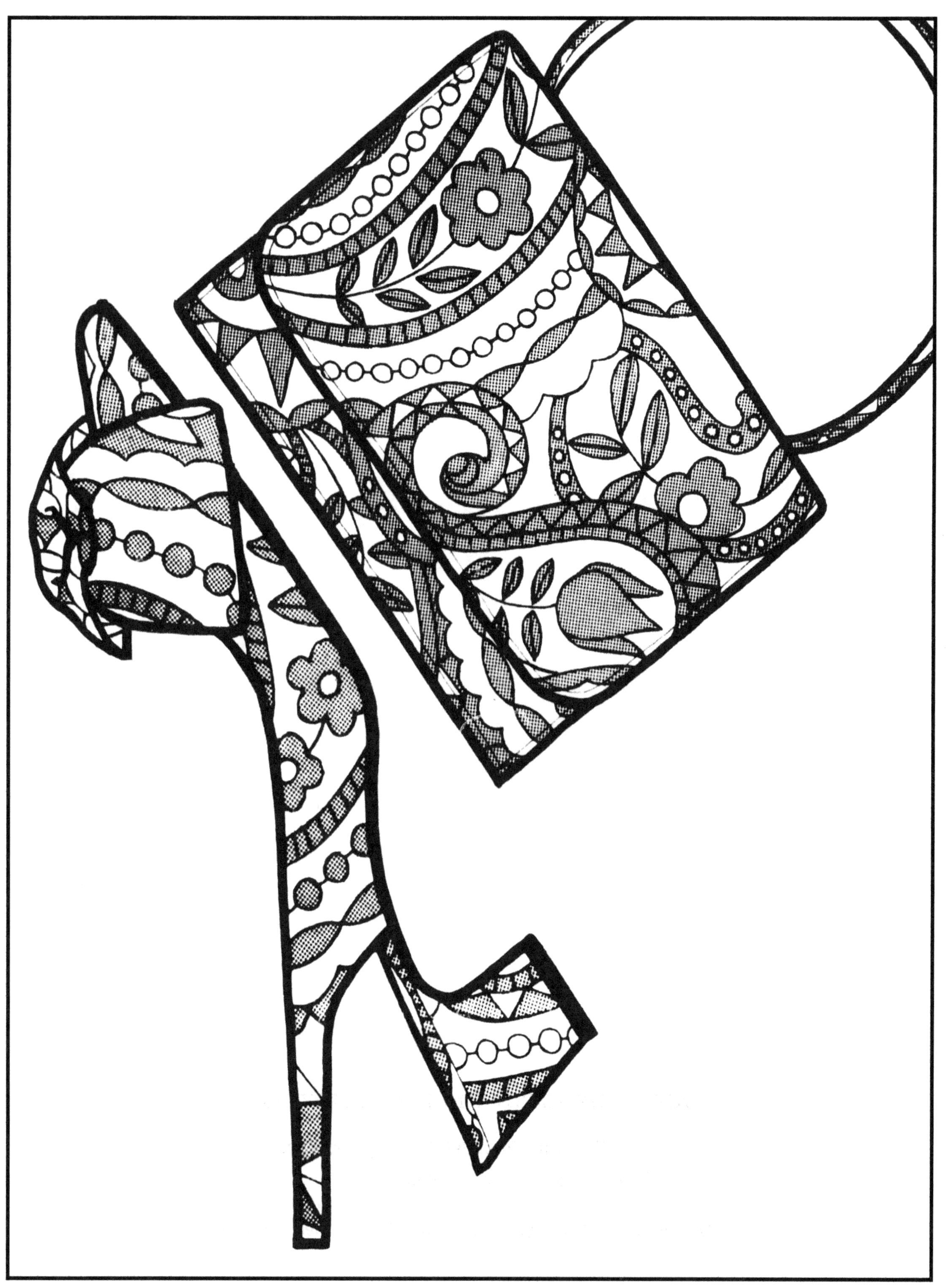

ABOUT THE ILLUSTRATION ON THE REVERSE

Original publication: Philadelphia Inquirer (Pennsylvania)
Publication date: April 3, 1968

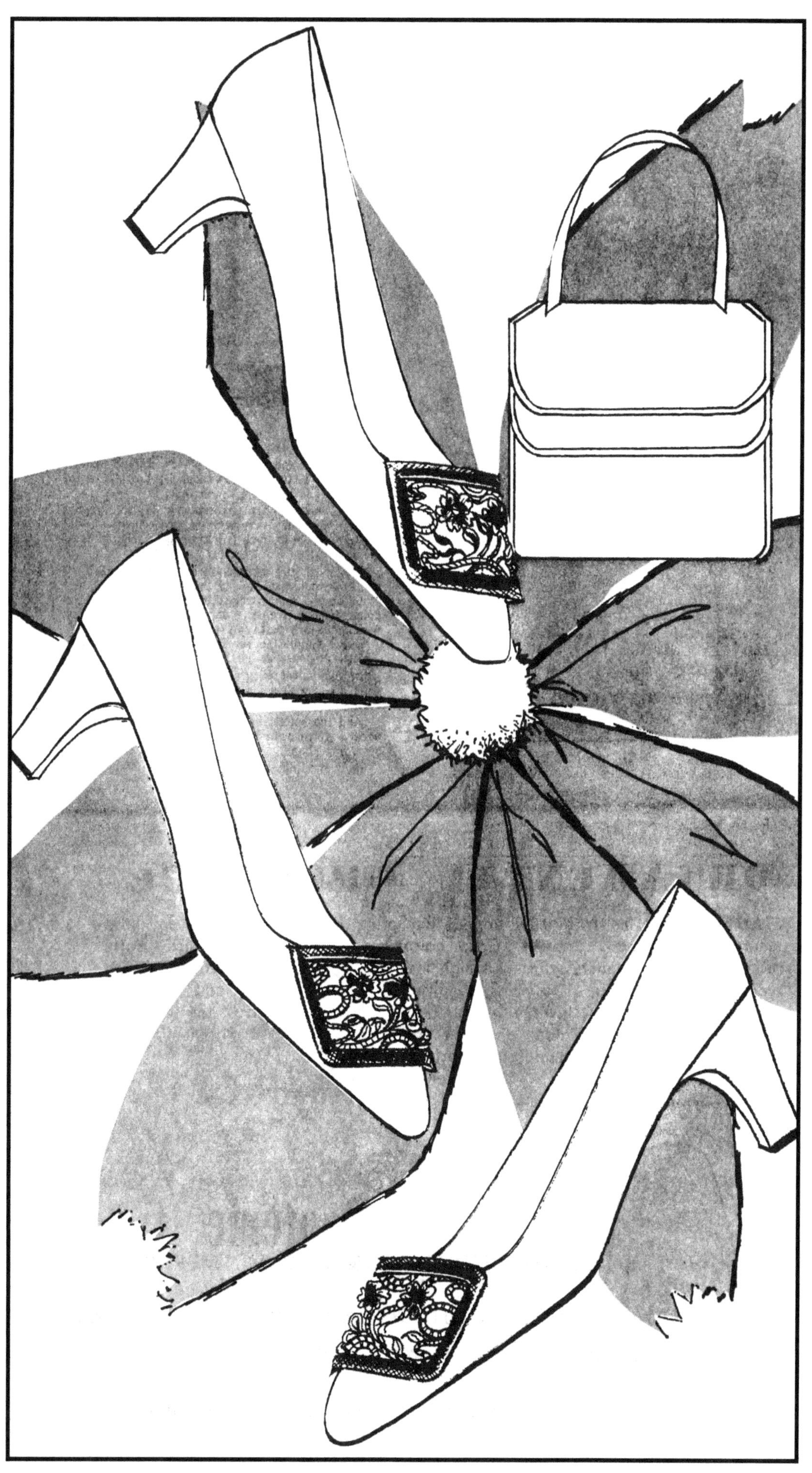

ABOUT THE ILLUSTRATION ON THE REVERSE

Original publication: The Tennessean (Nashville, Tennessee)
Publication date: March 2, 1969

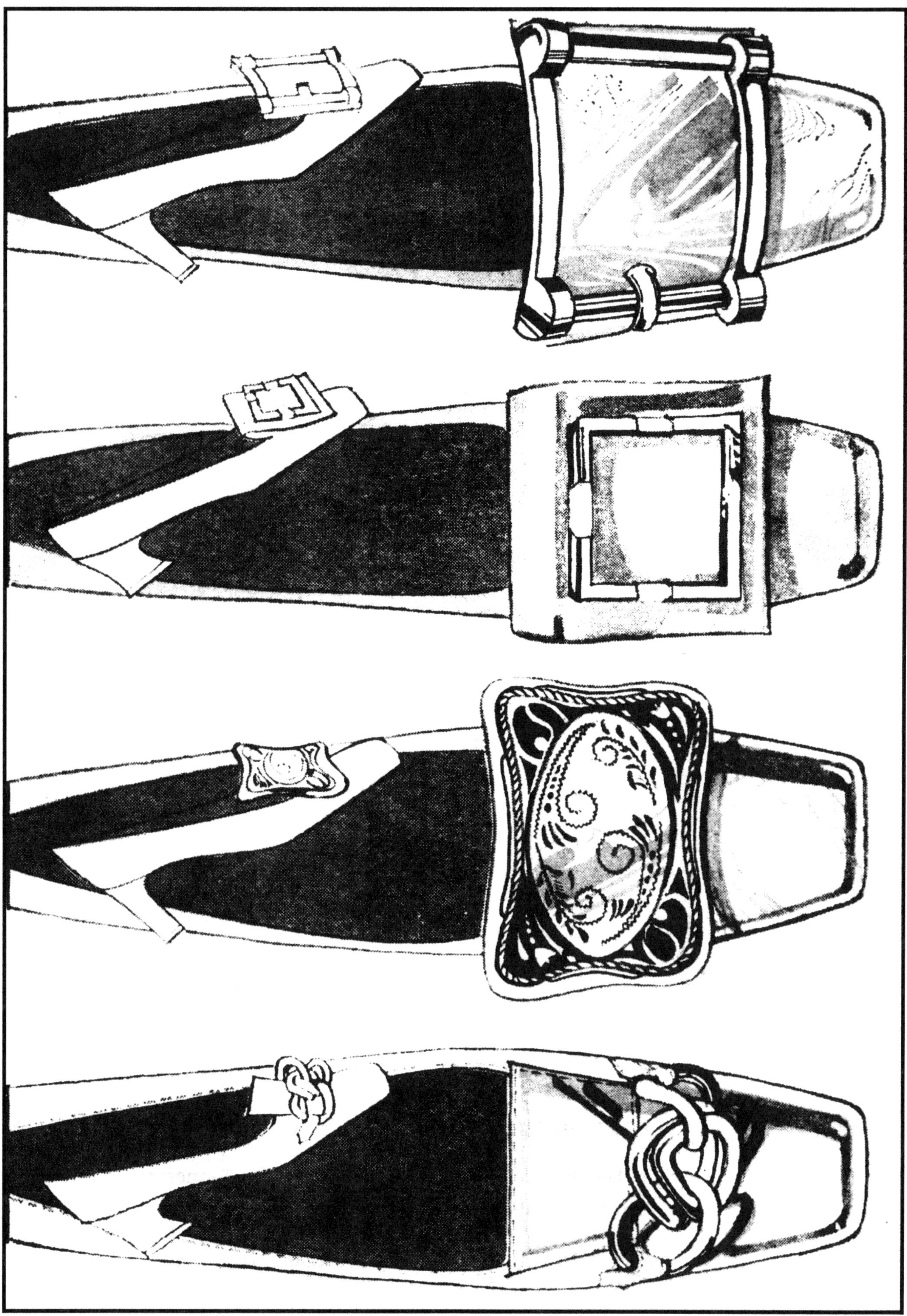

ABOUT THE ILLUSTRATION ON THE REVERSE

Original publication: The Tennessean (Nashville, Tennessee)

Publication date: March 2, 1969

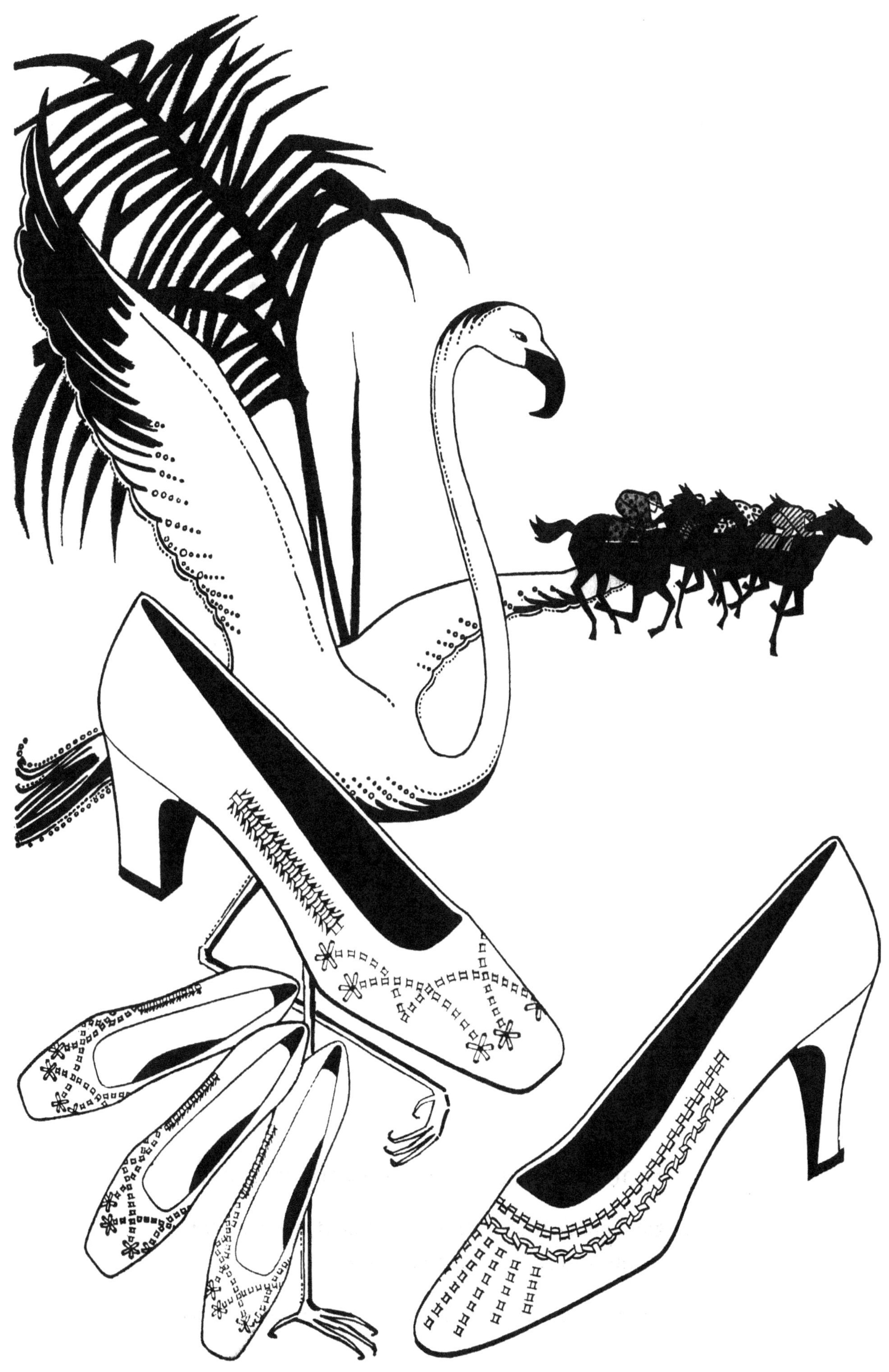

ABOUT THE ILLUSTRATION ON THE REVERSE

Original publication: The Orlando Sentinel (Florida)
Publication date: March 2, 1969

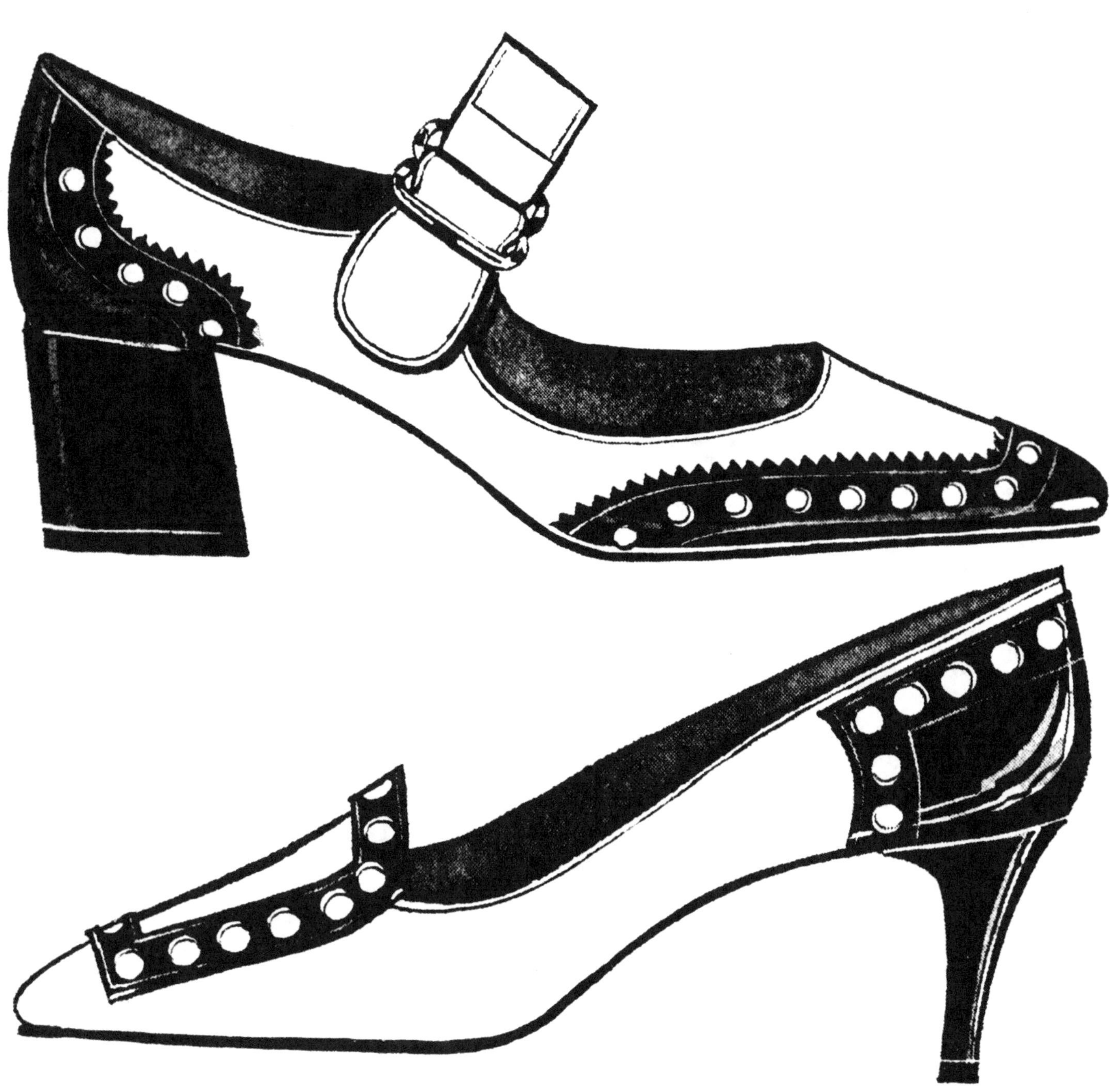

ABOUT THE ILLUSTRATION ON THE REVERSE

Original publication: The Tennessean (Nashville, Tennessee)
Publication date: March 9, 1969

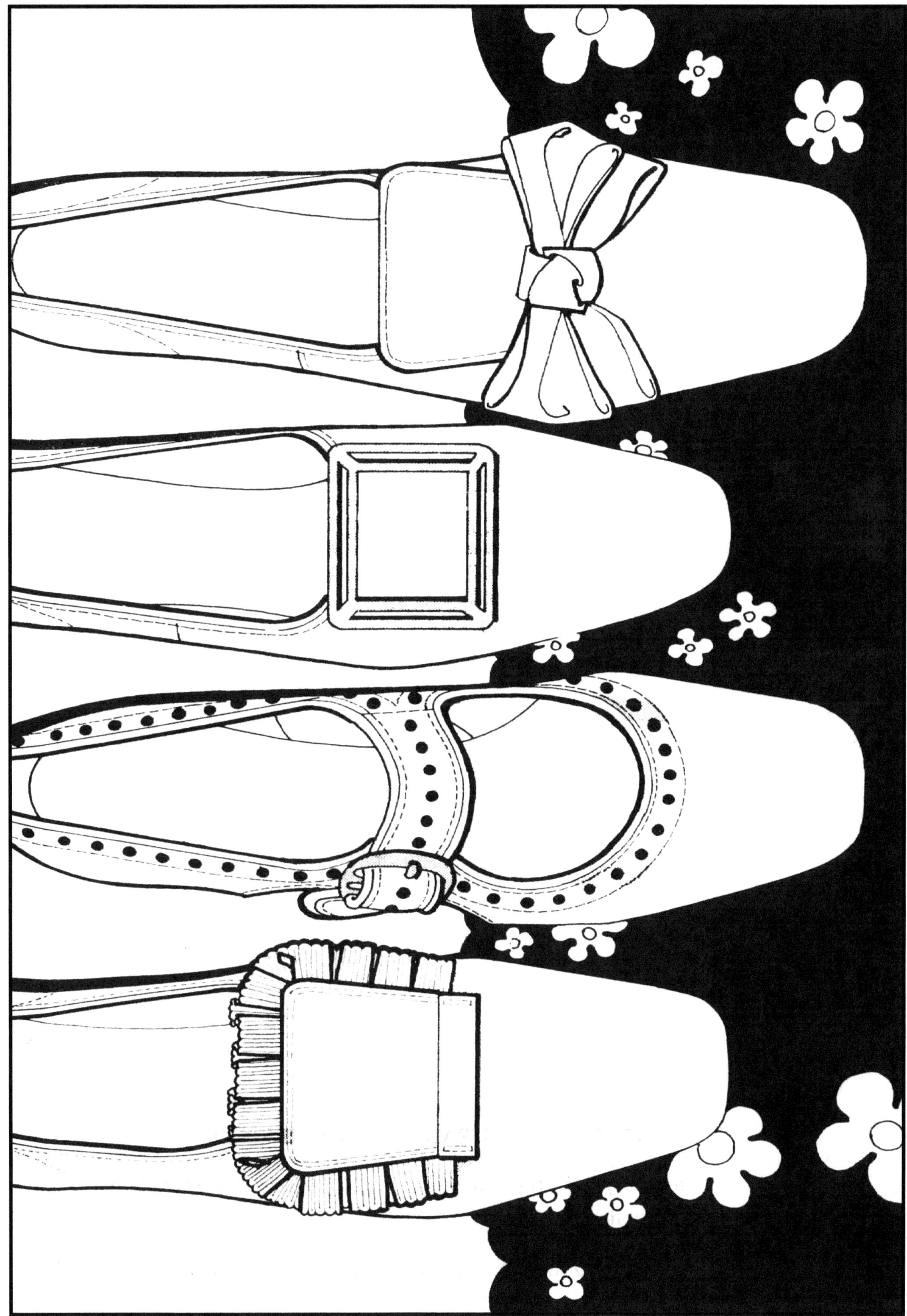

ABOUT THE ILLUSTRATION ON THE REVERSE

Original publication: Democrat and Chronicle (Rochester, NY)
Publication date: March 7, 1969

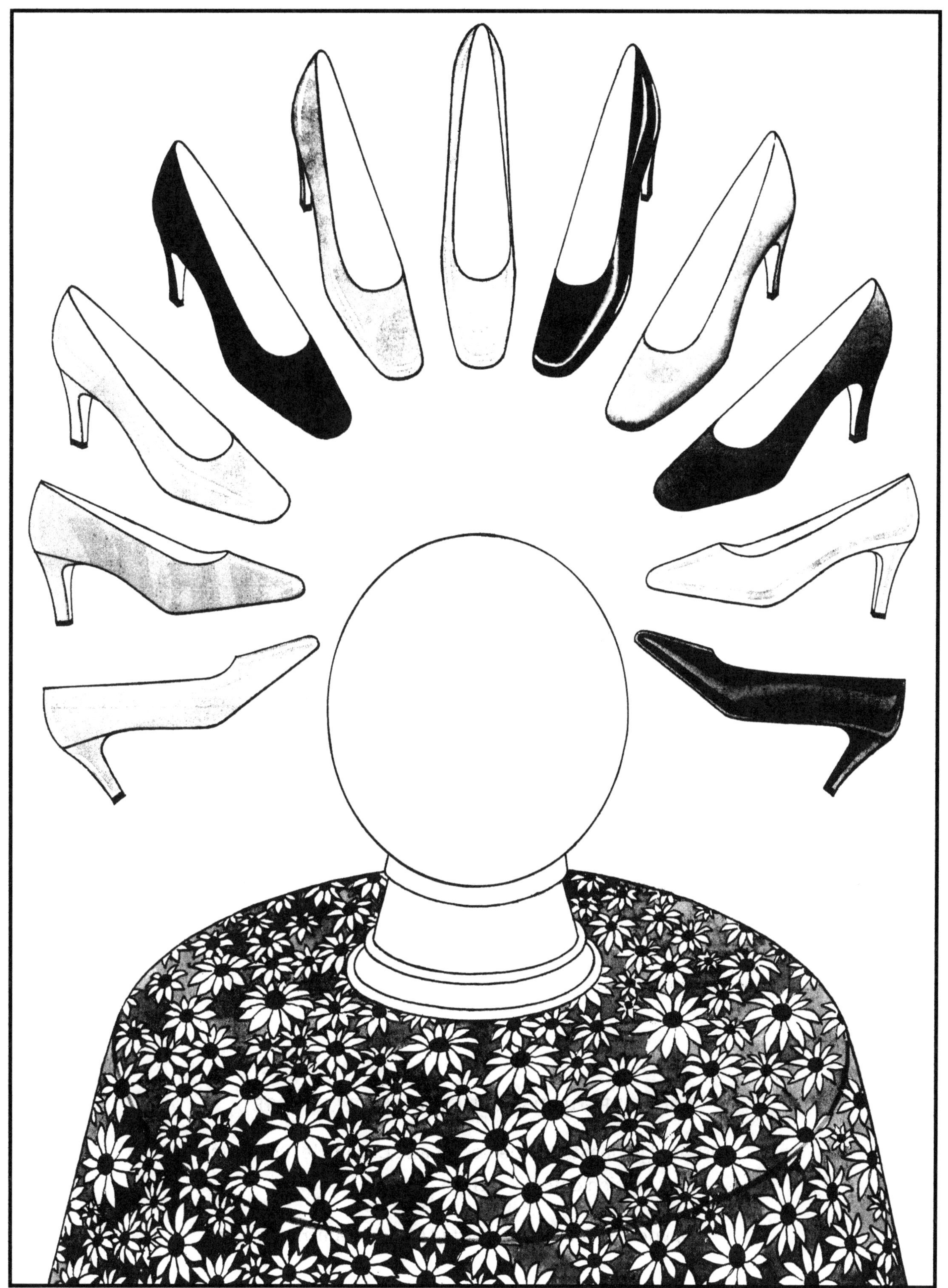

ABOUT THE ILLUSTRATION ON THE REVERSE

Original publication: Democrat and Chronicle (Rochester, NY)
Publication date: March 16, 1969

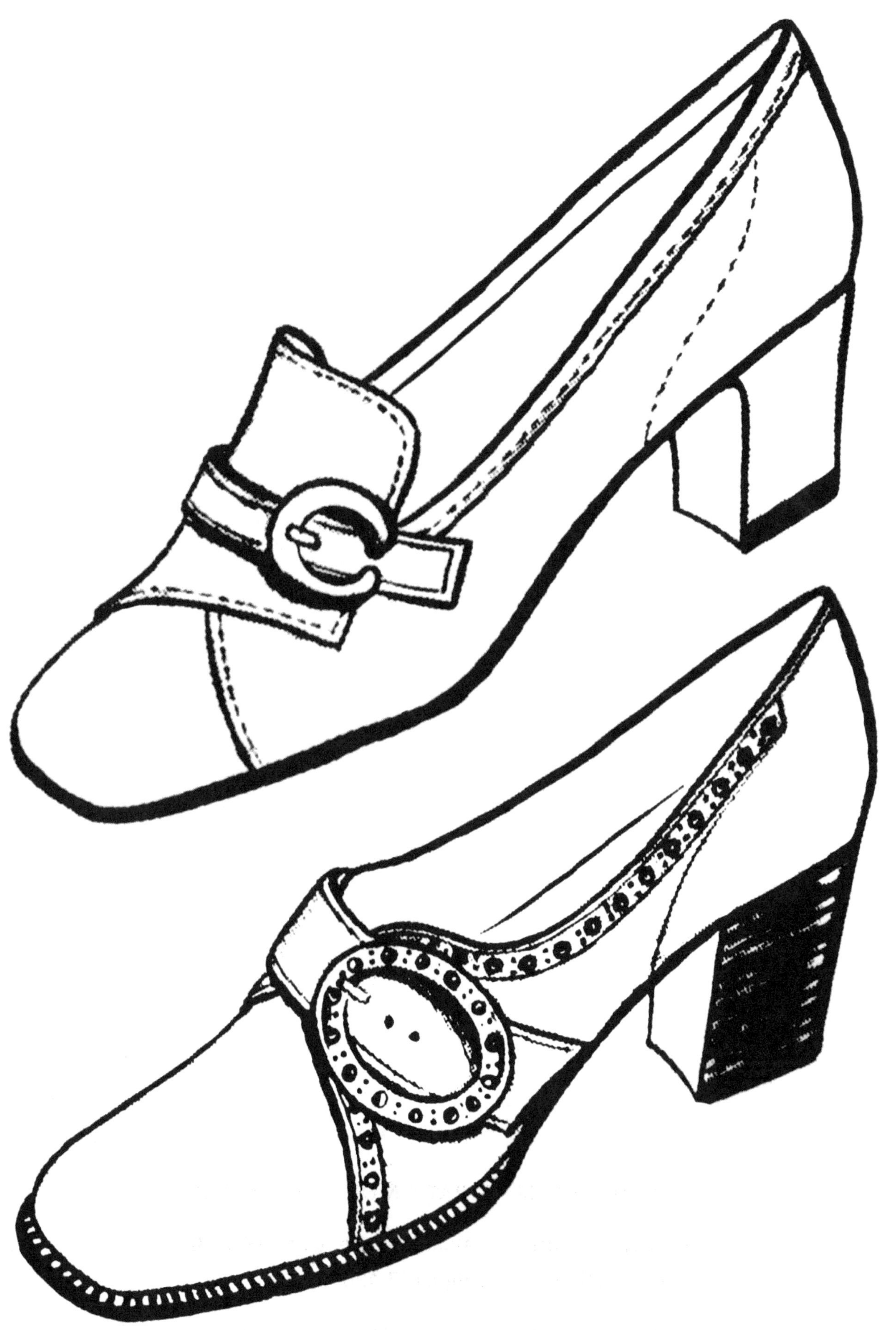

ABOUT THE ILLUSTRATION ON THE REVERSE

Original publication: Tallahassee Democrat (Florida)
Publication date: August 17, 1969

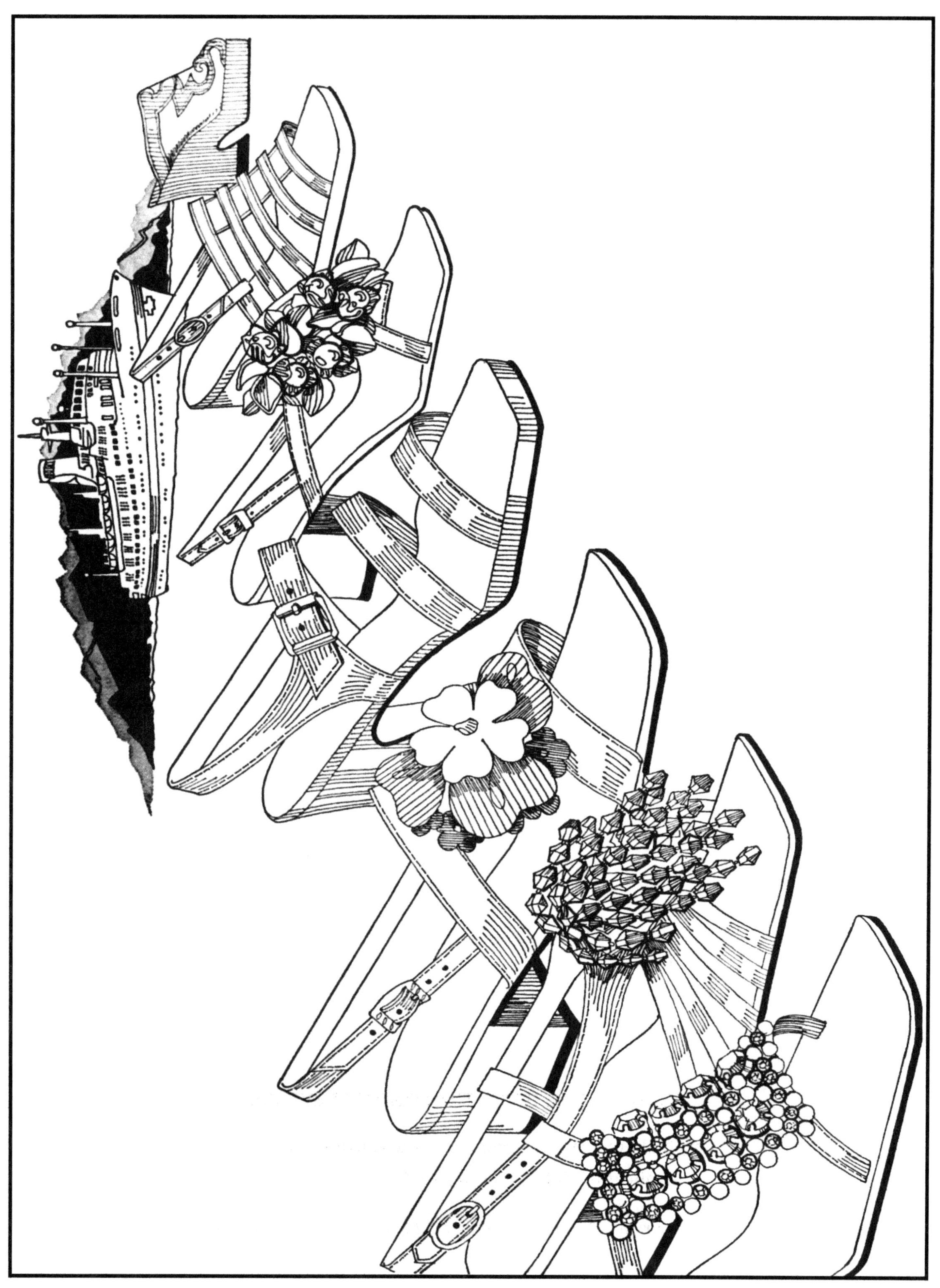

ABOUT THE ILLUSTRATION ON THE REVERSE

Original publication: Democrat and Chronicle (Rochester, NY)
Publication date: January 14, 1970

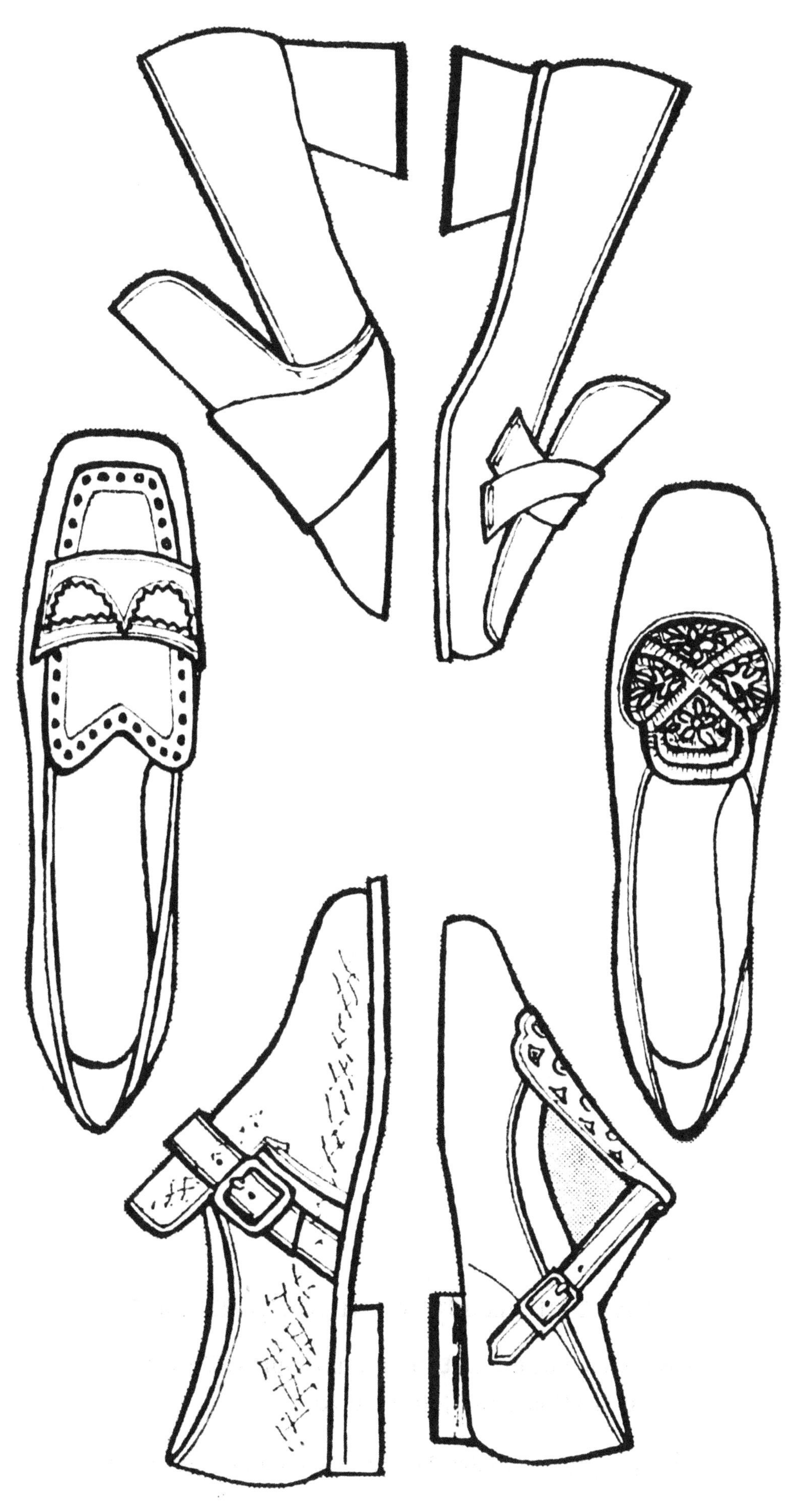

ABOUT THE ILLUSTRATION ON THE REVERSE

Original publication: San Antonio Express (Texas)
Publication date: July 26, 1970

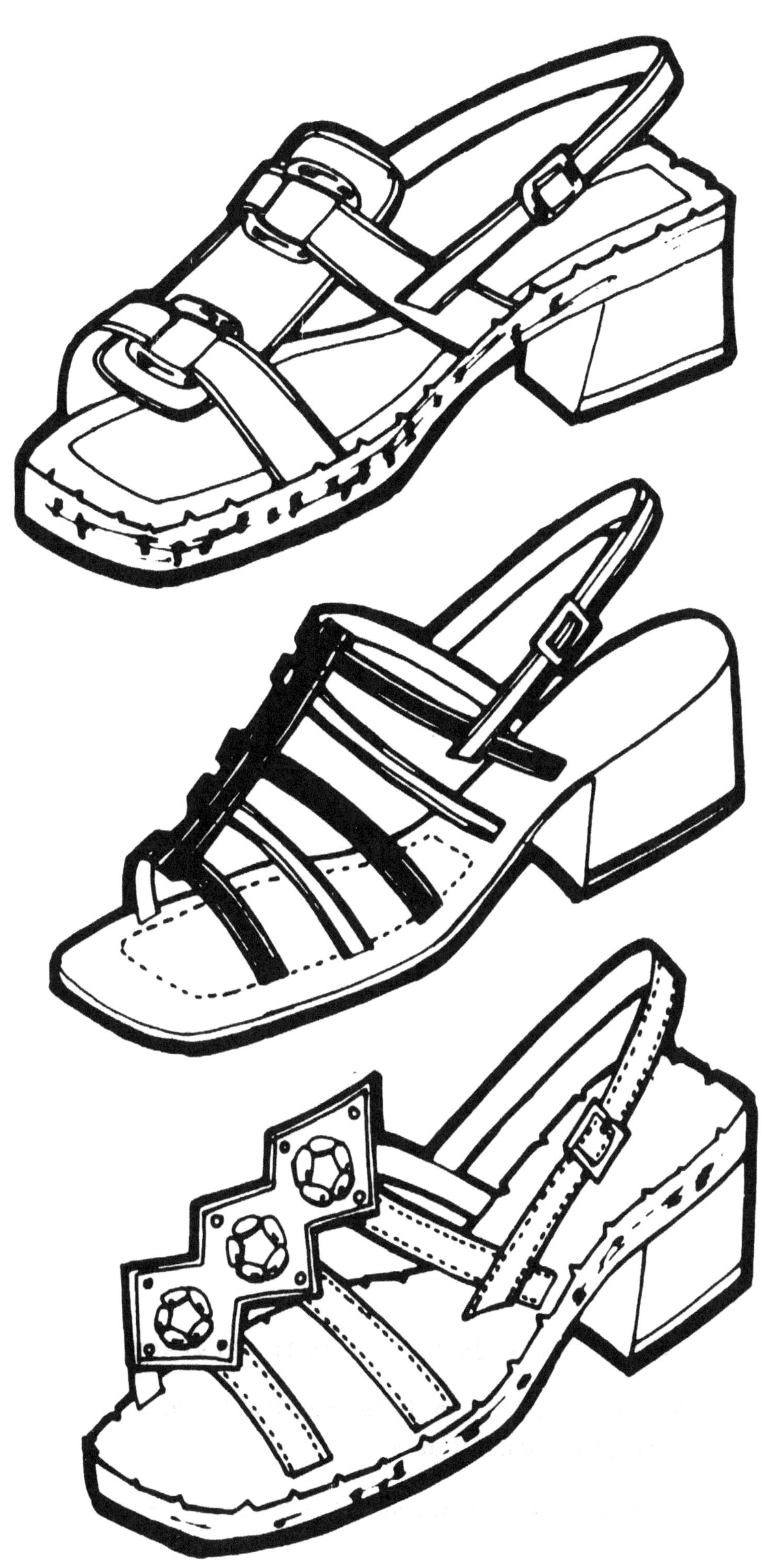

ABOUT THE ILLUSTRATION ON THE REVERSE

Original publication: The Palm Beach Post (Florida)
Publication date: March 31, 1971

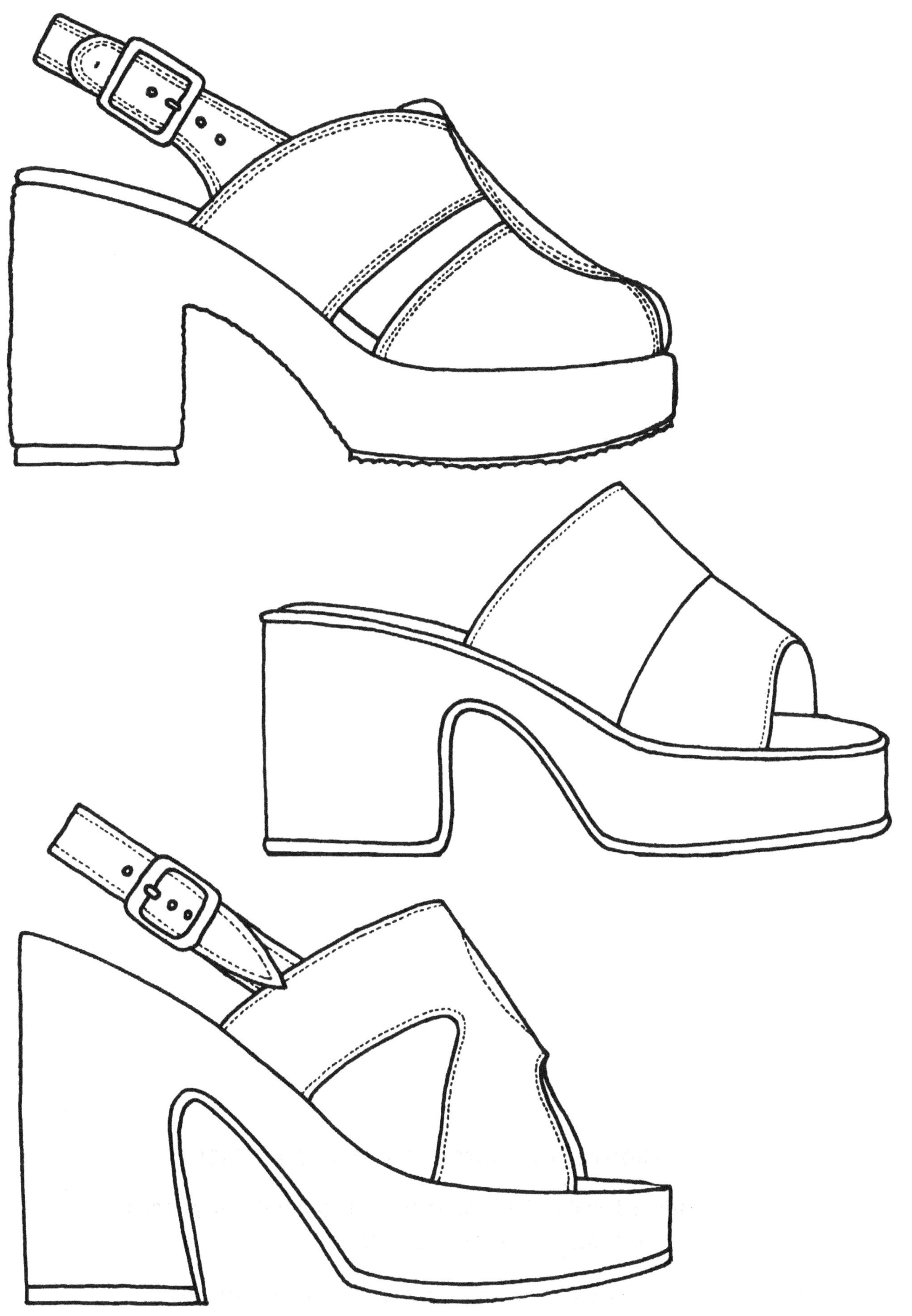

ABOUT THE ILLUSTRATION ON THE REVERSE

Original publication: Philadelphia Inquirer (Pennsylvania)
Publication date: May 13, 1973

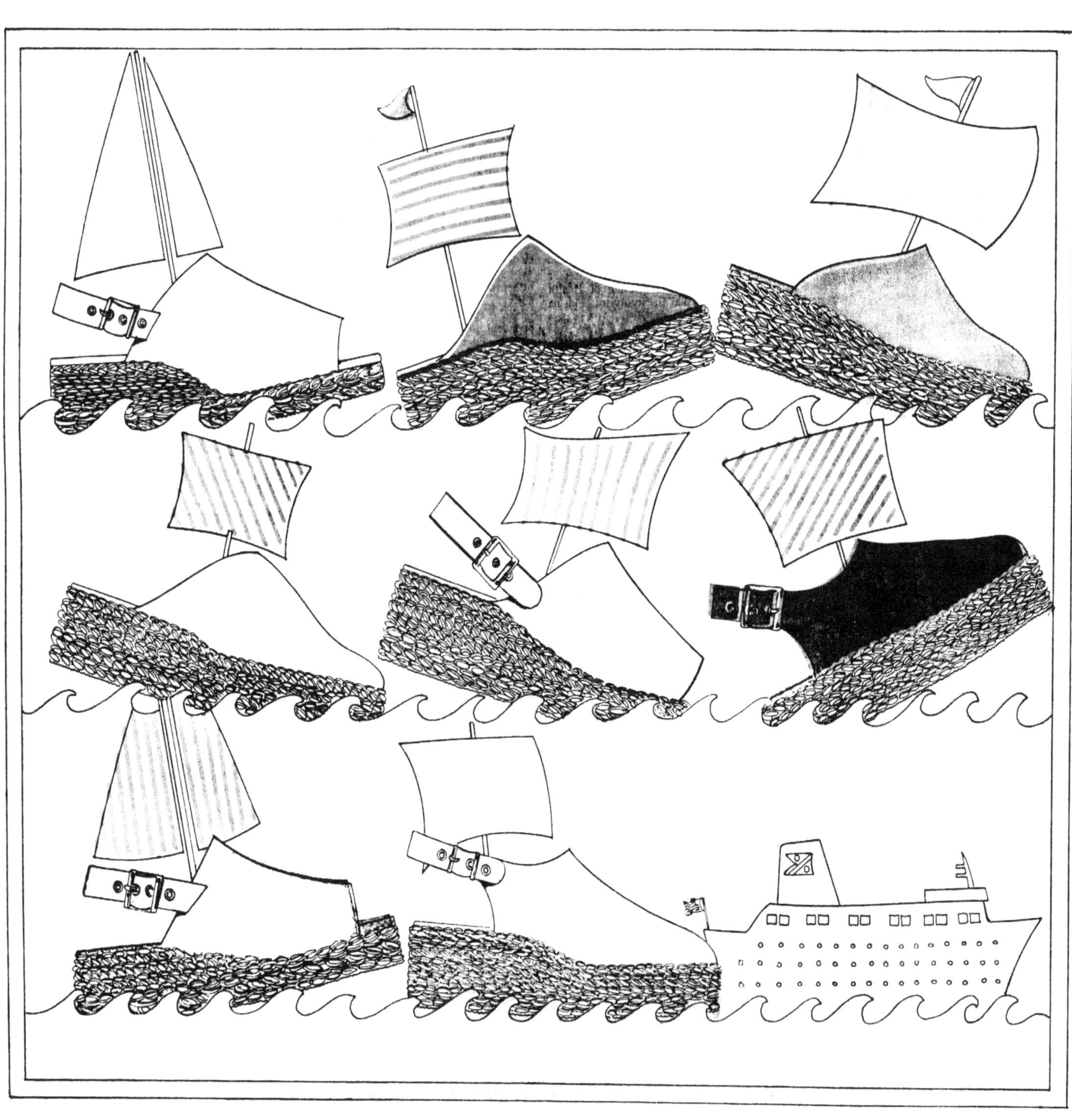

ABOUT THE ILLUSTRATION ON THE REVERSE

Original publication: The Orlando Sentinel (Florida)
Publication date: December 16, 1973

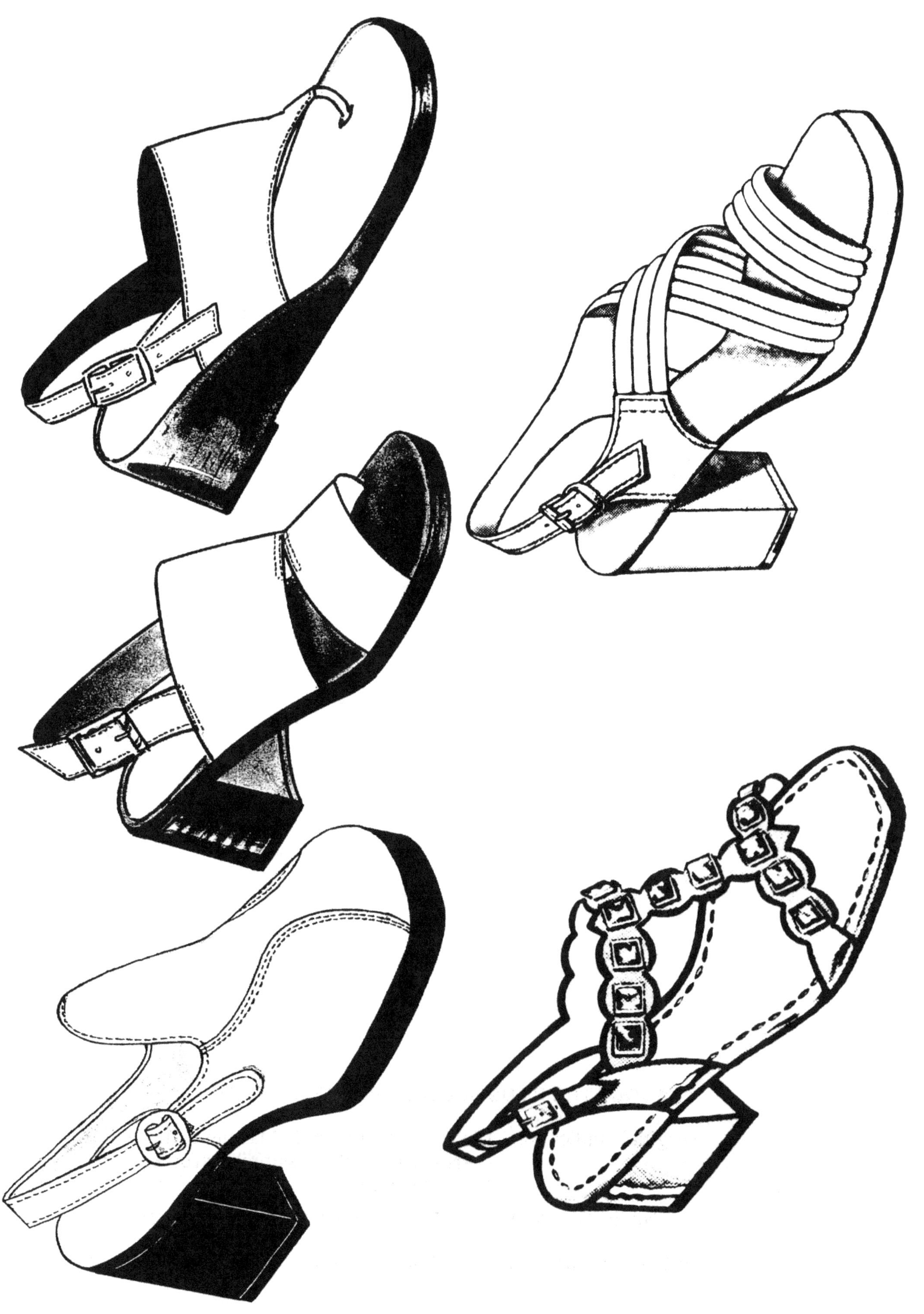

ABOUT THE ILLUSTRATION ON THE REVERSE

Original publication: Clockwise from top: La Marque Times (Texas); Clarion Ledger (Mississippi), Akron Beacon Journal (Ohio)

Publication date: May 17, 1973; April 4, 1974; March 9, 1973

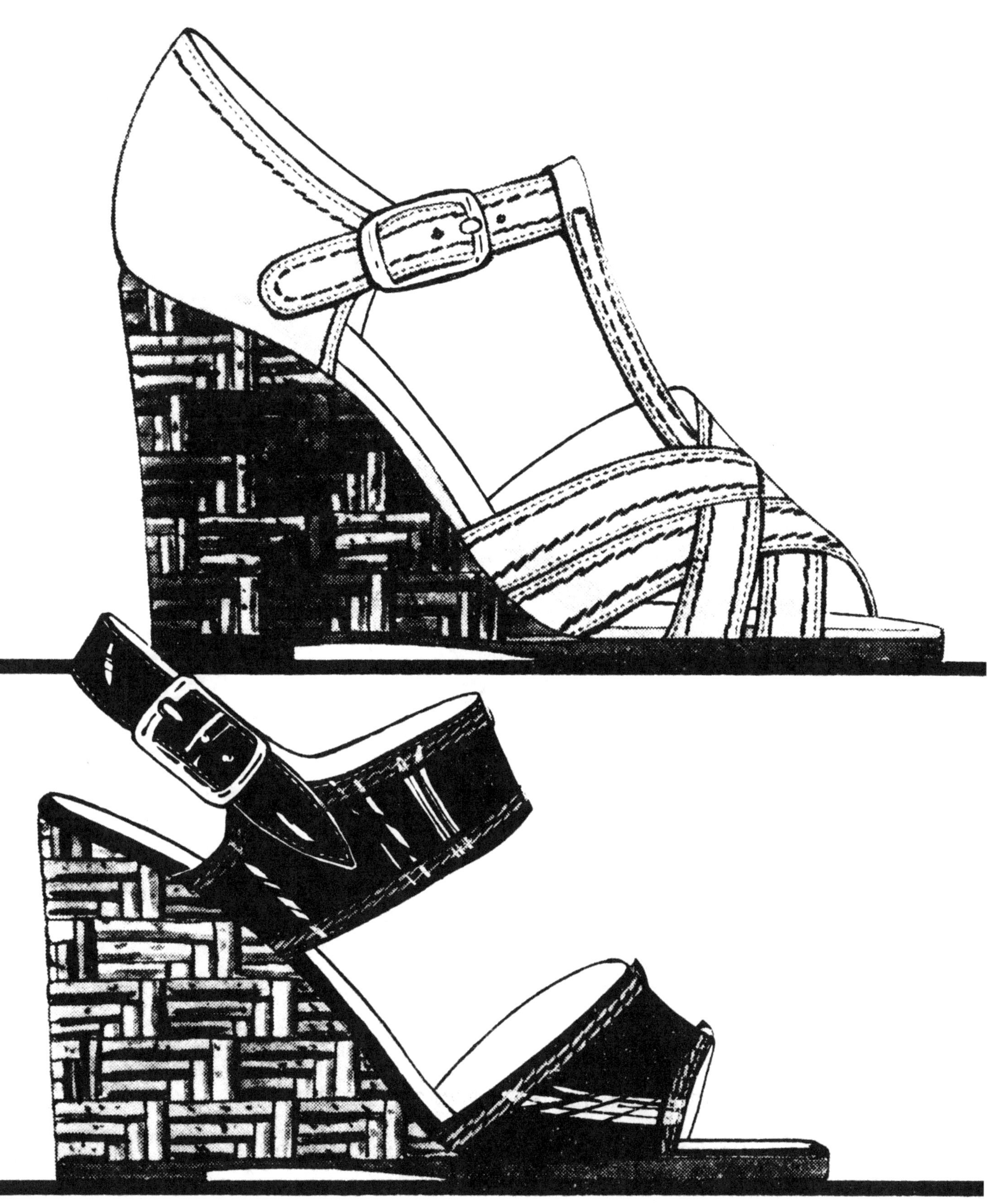

ABOUT THE ILLUSTRATION ON THE REVERSE

Original publication: San Antonio Express (Texas)
Publication date: January 8, 1976

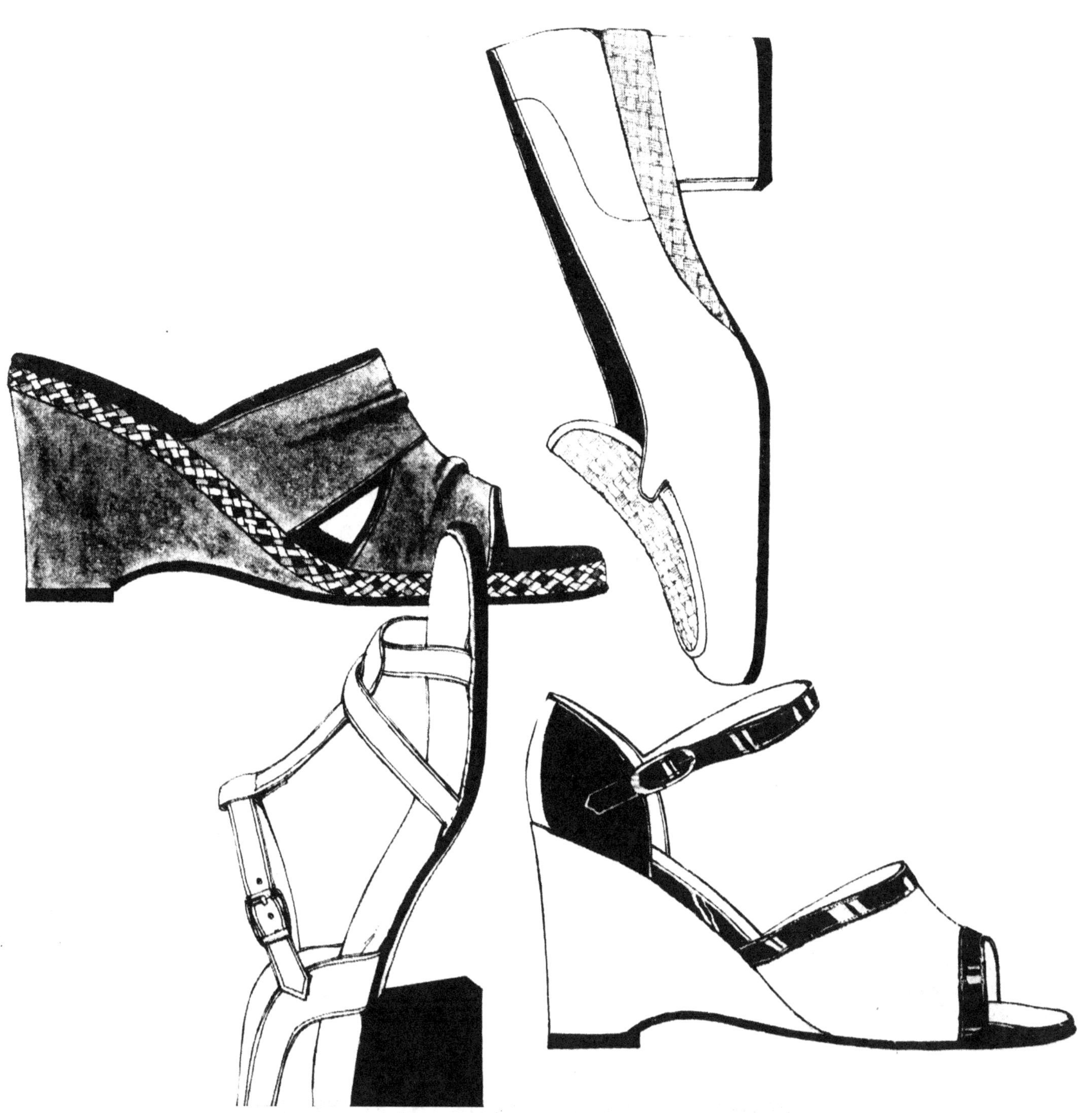

ABOUT THE ILLUSTRATION ON THE REVERSE

Original publication: San Antonio Express (Texas)
Publication date: January 18, 1976

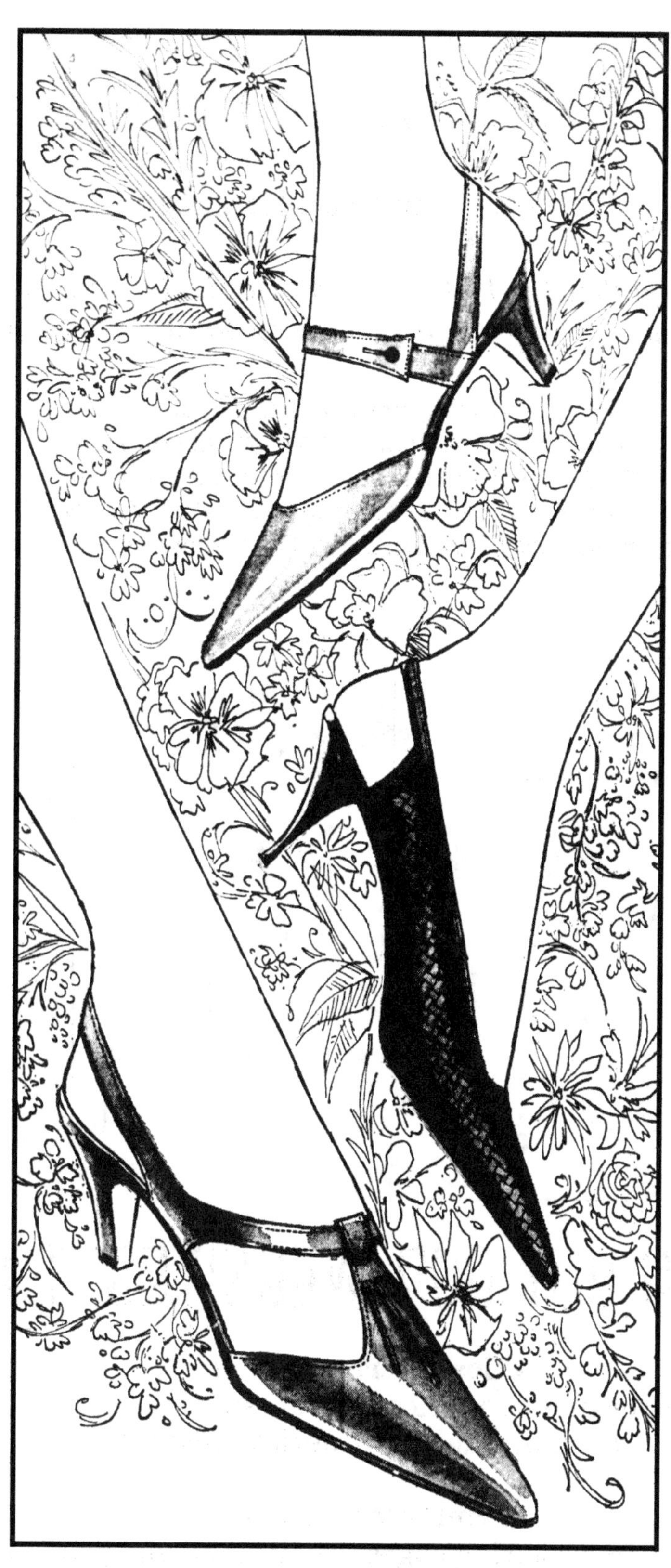

THE END

LIKE THIS BOOK? WE HAVE OTHERS!

Look for our whole *Vintage Women: Adult Coloring Book* series!

And for more coloring, see...

Large Print Adult Coloring Books (4 volumes)
Vintage Homes: Adult Coloring Books (3 volumes)

Other Synchronista titles:
Pantsuits: Scrapbook of a Style Revolution
The Beer Lover's Guide to Vintage Advertising
Something Old: Vintage Wedding Dress Fashion Look Book
All-In-One Pregnancy Calendar, Daily Countdown, Planner & Journal

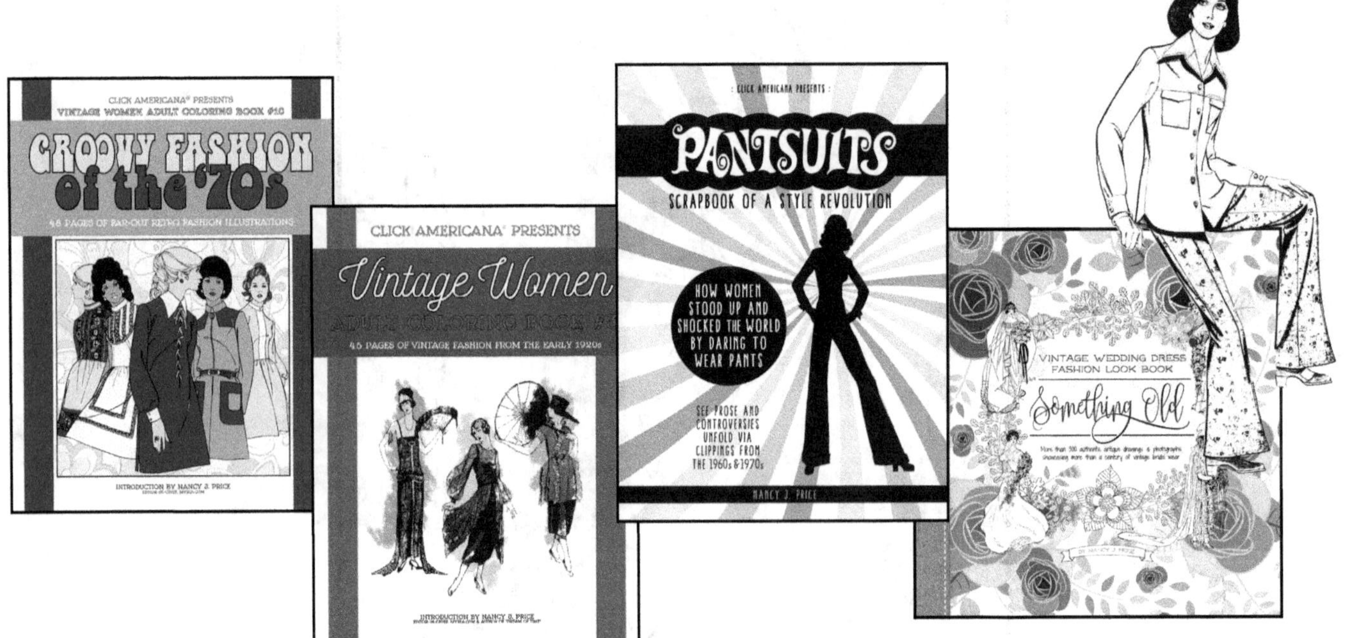

CHECK OUT OUR WEBSITES, TOO...

ClickAmericana.com
Thousands of articles, photos and vintage ads
from throughout American history.

PrintColorFun.com
Hundreds of free coloring pages to download and print at home.

Myria.com
Smart stuff for real life:
Health, parenting, psychology, science, tech, entertainment —
plus recipes, home decor & other good things.

BONUS! FREE BOOKMARKS

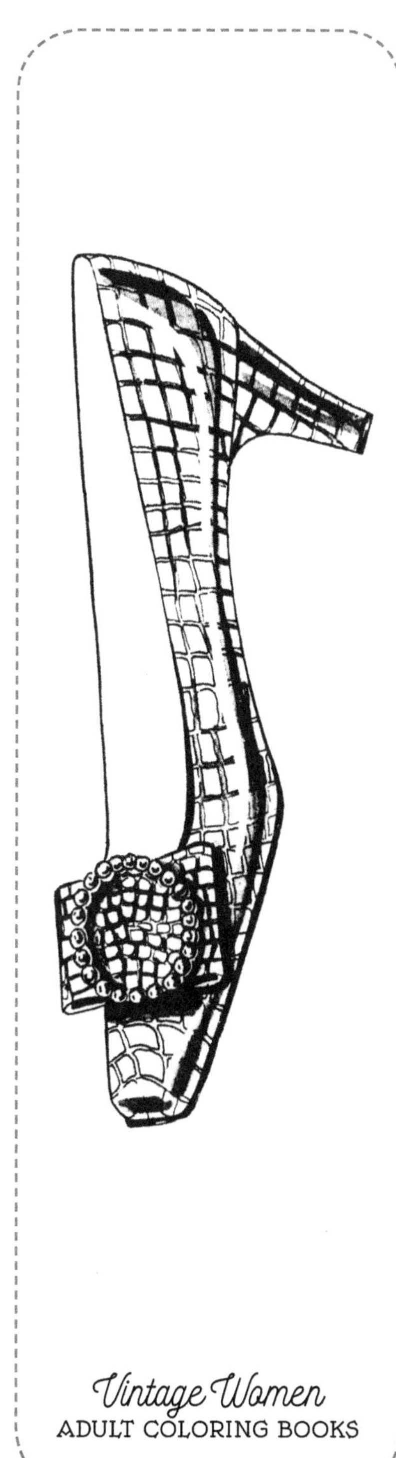

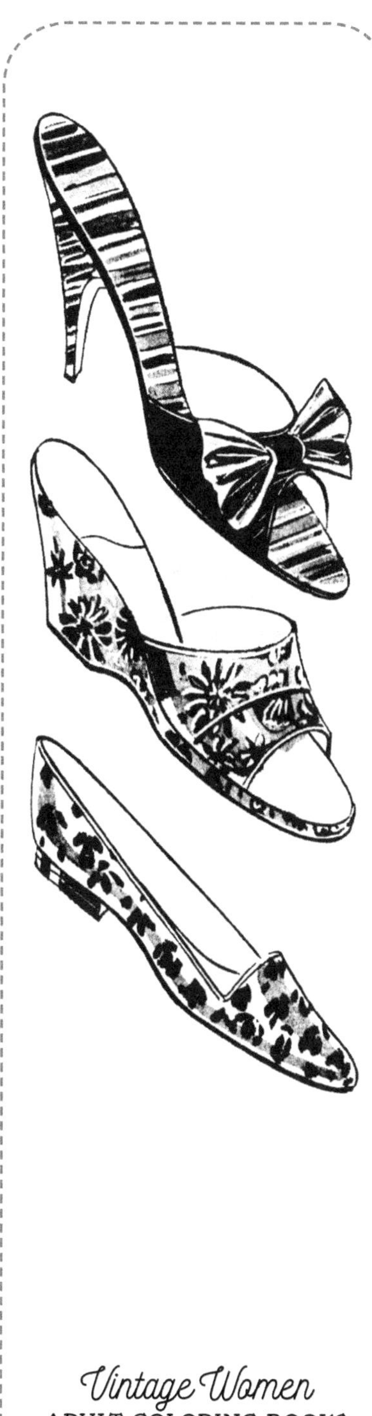

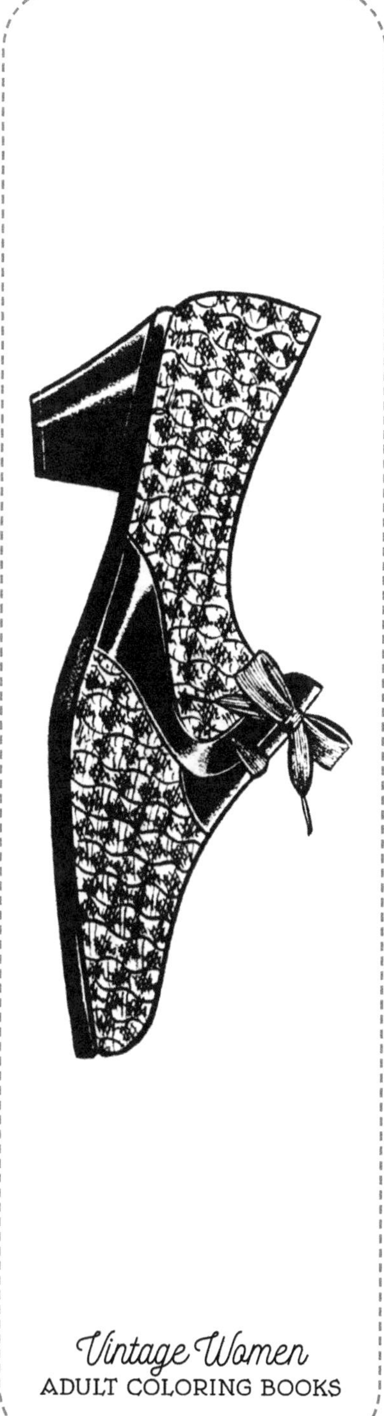

How to create durable bookmarks from the pictures above: 1) Color the images; 2) Cut just inside the dotted lines; 3) Laminate each bookmark or paste the cutout onto a thick piece of paper.

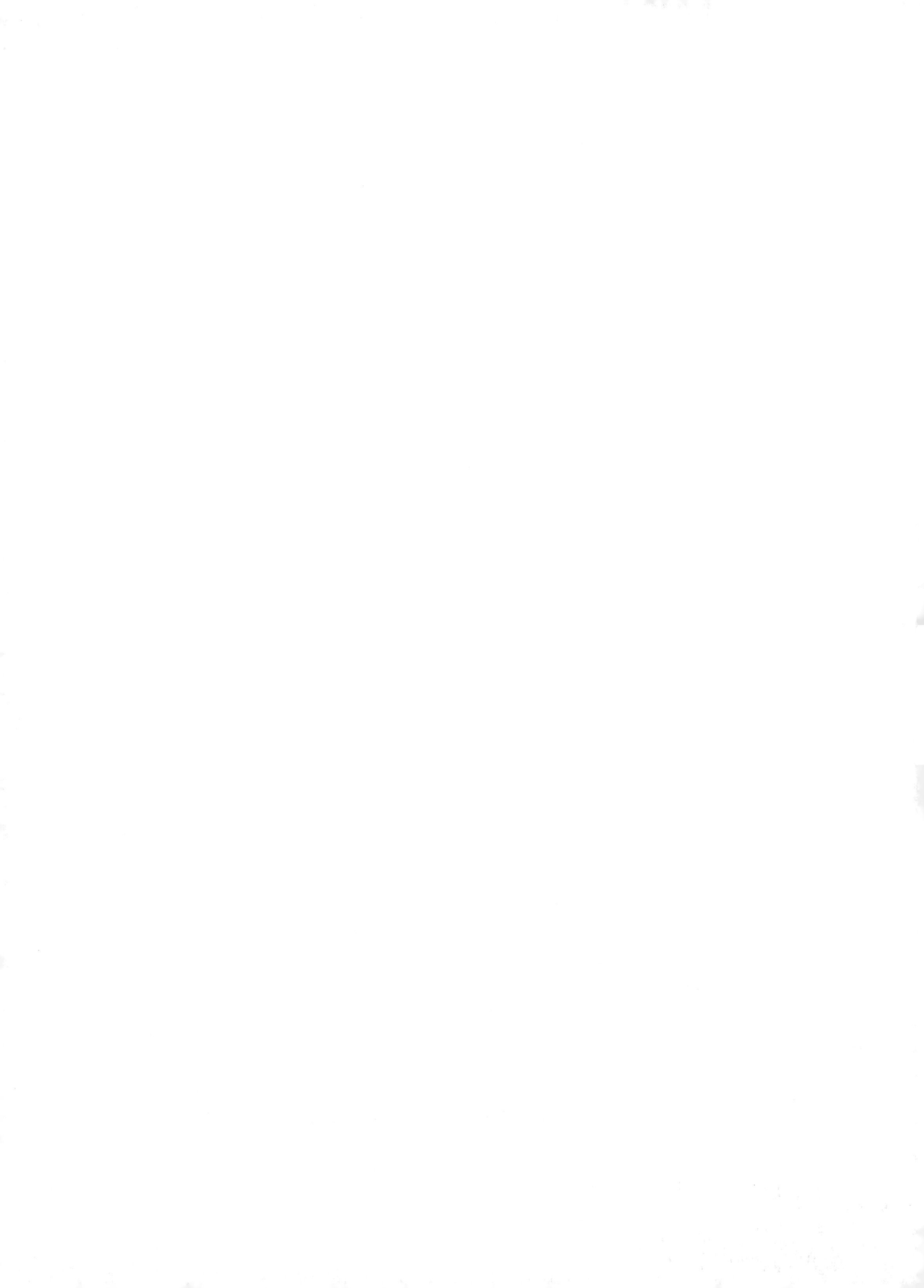

www.ingramcontent.com/pod-product-compliance
Lightning Source LLC
LaVergne TN
LVHW080923110826
845155LV00039B/196

* 9 7 8 1 9 4 4 6 3 3 6 2 2 *